White Feathers from Emmett

Dr. Sue Clifton
and
Jeff Gentry

BEAR SPIRIT PRESS

White Feathers from Emmett
Copyright © 2022 Dr. Sue Clifton and Jeff Gentry

All rights reserved under International and Pan-American Copyright Conventions. Published by Bear Spirit Press.

No part of this book may be reproduced or transmitted in any form or by any means, graphic, electronic, or mechanical, including photocopying, recording, taping, or by any information storage or retrieval system, without the permission in writing from Bear Spirit Press.

This book is a work of fiction. Names, characters, places and incidents are products of the author's imagination or are used fictitiously. Any resemblance to actual events or locales or persons, living or dead, is entirely coincidental.

Bear Spirit Press
ISBN-13: 978-1-77115-998-2

A Bear Spirit Press Second Edition April 25, 2022

To Mama
I miss you! Where's my white feather?
I love you,
Sudi

White Feathers from Emmett

Introduction

Part I   The Lynching of a Fun-Loving Boy

Chapter One   "Voices"
Chapter Two   "Knock, Knock!
                     "Who's There?"
                     "Emmett!"

Chapter Three   The Wolf Whistle
Chapter Four   The Abduction
Chapter Five   The Lynching
Chapter Six   The Trial and the "Confession"

Part II   White Feathers from Emmett

    Chapter Seven   White Feather #1
    Chapter Eight   White Feather #2
    Chapter Nine   Voices of Children and
                                             White Feather #3

    Chapter Ten   A Psychic Visits the Delta
    Chapter Eleven   Final Feather Falls
    Chapter Twelve   Summary of Scenarios

Conclusion
Photo Journal
About Cover Art
YouTube List
Works Consulted

A Few Words from Dr. Sue

My Writing Partner

Writing about Emmett Till is rewarding in so many ways. From my first day in the Delta visiting the Emmett Till sites, I have felt connected to Emmett, a bond increasing in emotional attachment each time I go. But with the emotionalism comes realization. Describing the macabre details of one of the most horrific child murders in history will absolutely hurt too much, making it NOT possible for me as a mother and a grandmother to write even as the author of this book. But, just as Mamie Till-Mobley wanted the world to "see what they had done to her boy" and left his casket open for viewing in Chicago, I feel obligated to make my readers feel, really feel, Emmett's pain and suffering at the hands of his savage murderers. I need help! The answer to my dilemma lives several states away in Connecticut—my "answer" stands ready!

Jeff Gentry is a gifted writer who just happens to be my son. His forte is describing gruesome scenes using graphic imagery, allowing each reader not only to see the horror but to feel the emotions and pain of the victim(s). This is not the first time Jeff has helped me with a book and I doubt it will be the last. In one of my novels, Jeff wrote a series of letters written from the perspective of a soldier in Vietnam, describing battle scenes so real readers could feel the bullets zip past their ears or smell the stench of death whether of fellow soldiers or innocent village children. Each reader was allowed to live vicariously through the young soldier as he moved through his own emotional battles from excitement to fear, from battle fatigue to despondency.

Thank you, Jeff, for co-writing this book with me. Once again, you saved your mother and this time you will receive proper credit with your name on the cover and title page. Reading the chapter on

Emmett's torture and murder will certainly leave readers feeling the young boy's pain and, hopefully, will instill in each reader a strong sense of the injustice so prevalent in the Jim Crow era.

About *White Feathers from Emmett*

My intention in writing *White Feathers from Emmett* is not to summarize everything known or written about Emmett Till. So many more capable researchers, authors, historians, civil rights advocates, and family members have done the subject far more justice than I could ever do. Many events surrounding Emmett's life and death are described in this book but with succinctness—just enough to give this book the historical structure needed for narrative flow, to keep the reader (and the authors) on track, and hopefully, to make it more credible.

In addition to historical research, paranormal investigative techniques were used at five major Emmett Till sites in the Mississippi Delta with emphasis on three sites. Voices, sounds, and activity were recorded at each place using a simple Sony video camera. No special equipment of the type used on TV "ghost hunting" shows was used with the exception of a K-2 meter which measures electromagnetic energy.

Where noted, please watch the YouTube videos to hear and see activity recorded in the context in which it was filmed. I hope you will be as amazed as I was when I played the footage back and heard what I believe to be the voices of Emmett Till, Henry Lee Loggins, a few unidentified male voices, and one very happy little girl spirit.

Introduction
Not Just "Another Book on Emmett Till"

I sit in the courtroom in Sumner, Mississippi, the same courtroom where in September 1955, brothers J.W. Milam and Roy Bryant were acquitted of the murder of fourteen-year-old Emmett Till, a boy from Chicago who knew only northern "city ways." The old courthouse, now listed on the National Register of Historic Places, stands still and silent, guarded only by a single confederate soldier remaining on guard in the courtyard. The soldier, like my ancestors who fought for the Confederacy, is no longer in a position of pride and hero worship like in the past. His very being is threatened by present day haters who feel he symbolizes much more than "preservation of state's rights." Perhaps, he even looks a little remorseful as if he is being held responsible for the acquittal of the two child murderers over sixty years ago in this old courthouse. The stately but "ghostly" old building looks and feels every bit as it did in that day—held captive in a perpetual time warp. It is September 1955—FOREVER!

Sitting at the bench where Judge Swango's gavel pounded out control of the emotionally charged audience, I am transported back to 1955. The vibes pulsate like a heart feeding a mind gone mad! I cast my eyes over the old auditorium seats and feel the tension of two hundred sweat-drenched, white males as they watch, their expressions etched in support of murderers J.W. Milam and Roy Bryant. I wish I could tell the white spectators their claiming the two "peckerwoods" as their own will be short-lived—to be overshadowed by J.W. Milam's confession a few weeks later to journalist William Bradford Huie for $4000 paid to the brothers to "confess the truth" for an article in *Look* Magazine.

An imaginary fog hangs in the ceiling like hoarfrost as the crowd of men below puff away on their filter-less cigarettes, or switch from chewing on stub ends to smoking Old Stogies, adding to the effluence. But today the fans remain stationary and silent—not whipping the thick miasma into toxic clouds as their blades once did. The fans, obsolete except for their place in history, have been outperformed by cold air conditioning, not original but necessary for the mass of tourists who visit in the present paying homage to the boy who died too young—too violently.

Fifty or more black spectators sit in the back row or lean against the walls, some inching their way closer to open windows but being careful not to get in the way of white onlookers, all hoping to catch a breeze albeit a scorching one. The courtroom can hold no more curious watchers; its walls bulge close to bursting filled with jurors, lawyers, spectators, journalists from both black and white newspapers and magazines, television reporters, families of the accused, and the family of Emmett Till—including his brave mother Mamie.

Casting glances around me, I breathe heavily as reality returns. The courtroom is empty, devoid of crowds of perspiring bodies, of tobacco smoke, and even of the brutal heat and humidity of Mississippi's summer. The keys on my laptop dance with emotion as I sit at Judge Swango's bench, and even though I am alone in the old courtroom, I experience no trepidation UNTIL…

One of the big double doors opens making a terrific noise! My eyes dart from my computer screen to the back of the courtroom and I stare at the door, watching it open and then bang closed. No one enters—at least no one I can see! No footfalls pound the wood floor; no chair squeaks as if pulled down for seating. But my senses tell me I am not alone.

After perhaps a minute of total silence, I shrug my shoulders and continue to write, wondering in the back of my mind if this could be the shadowy presence I caught in a video a couple of months earlier at the head of the table in the jury deliberation room. Or perhaps it is the male who lingers in the courtroom, enjoying any "live" person who enters—the man who yelled, "Wait!" when Bill Foster, our guide on our first visit here, turned out the lights signaling our departure. Or, could it be the burly white male with the southern drawl, the gruff, controlling "officer of the court", or of Tallahatchie County, who orders my friend Belinda, "Get off the phone!"

Watch the YouTube video: "Voices of the Courthouse: Sumner, Mississippi" https://youtu.be/f7g7mYhbUzc *for these surreal experiences.*

1955

I was ten-years-old when Emmett was murdered, but unlike thousands of other children, I was never traumatized by seeing the monstrous, mutilated and bloated face of Emmett in JET Magazine, September 15, 1955, edition, displaying the young teen in his casket in Chicago. My parents never warned me to look whites in the eyes, to move off the sidewalk when whites approached, to always say "sir" and "ma'am" with eyes lowered in subservience, and to take whatever negativity whites dished out, including physical punishment, even if I'd done nothing wrong. But then—I was a white girl growing up one county over from where this horrendous crime took place. Truth is, I never heard of Emmett Till until I was in college in the 1960's.

Now, I sit here at my computer attempting to describe the torture and murder of this African American child who is the same age as some of my grandchildren. For the past few months, I have read much on the internet about Emmett's torture and murder and the subsequent miscarriage of justice. In addition, I have bought and read many books about the case and about the young boy Emmett, my mind seeking out and digesting primary sources such as *Simeon's Story: An Eye Witness Account of the Kidnapping of Emmett Till* by Simeon Wright with Herb Boyd; *Death of Innocence: The Story of the Hate Crime That Changed America* by Mamie Till-Mobley and Christopher Benson.

I have also read and/or used as research comprehensive

studies such as: *Emmett Till: The Murder That Shocked the World and Propelled the Civil Rights Movement* by Devery S. Anderson; *The Blood of Emmett Till* by Timothy B. Tyson. *(See "Works Consulted" at end of book).*

Many of these and other writers used superior investigative skills in researching Emmett's case. I found the works of Susan Orr-Klopfer and Bonnie Blue especially intriguing. Susan Orr-Klopfer took advantage of her move to the Delta with her husband who worked at Parchman Penitentiary as a psychologist. She interviewed countless witnesses, mostly elderly people who remembered the murder and who knew information, not only about Emmett's murder, but personal information about J.W. Milam and Roy Bryant. Klopfer worked on other civil rights cold cases as well as the Emmett Till case. Bonnie Blue interviewed J.W. Milam by telephone and gained his trust so well, he wanted to take the young interviewer and show her the sites where everything happened if she ever traveled to Mississippi. This never came to fruition because of J.W. Milam's death from cancer in 1977.

I watched over and over, *The Untold Story of Emmett Louis Till* by filmmaker Keith Beauchamp. Keith was Mamie Till-Mobley's friend and Keith was blessed with her support and encouragement in his own quest to fill in the gaps of missing information and to give a true account of Emmett's tragic story. Keith discovered many new angles to the murder and identified accomplices and witnesses never mentioned during the trial in 1955. When he was only twenty-two years old, Keith set out to make a movie about Emmett but after becoming friends with Mamie, Keith's main goal changed and his efforts were spent in securing the reopening of the Till case by the FBI. Keith accomplished this goal in 2004, unfortunately after Mamie's death. His documentary on Emmett's murder was instrumental in getting the case reopened.

Now Keith is my friend, and just as Keith became obsessed with investigating and researching Emmett's murder for the bulk of his adult life, I have become consumed by Emmett's story in my senior years. Emmett absorbs my every waking moment and keeps me awake at night, draining me of energy. At times, I feel I am going insane, unable to put him out of my thoughts. The more I learn, the hungrier I grow for FACTS, those details shrouded in secrecy, never shared completely or told the same way twice by some who knew firsthand, most of whom are now deceased. Total truth surrounding Emmett's murder remains elusive to even the most dedicated researchers, or grows in retelling much like the children's game of gossip.

The events between 2:00 AM and late morning, August 28, 1955, surrounding Emmett's kidnapping, torture, and murder, seem weighted down, much like the young boy's body when dumped in a muddy river with a heavy gin fan tied around his neck. But unlike Emmett's body that resurfaced after three days, most of the "gospel truth" remains sunken in the Tallahatchie River…eaten away by prehistoric alligator gars, their sharp teeth tearing away at certainties until only "holey" ambiguities remain. From time to time, fragments have surfaced and were quickly netted by those, like Keith Beauchamp, who care most about providing final justice for Emmett, Mamie, and the family.

As I prepared to visit the sites where Emmett was kidnapped, tortured, and murdered, I had no intention of turning this tragic but historical event into a paranormal investigation. I did, however, pack up my video camera knowing too well that all historical locations carry vibes from the past, an unusual and controversial way of arriving at possible truths but something I have experienced too much of in the last four years to dismiss as fantasy or delusion.

Things happen to me—steppingstones seem magically, or Divinely, placed in my path, leading me to important events. In 1955, I was but a child in Mississippi when Emmett the child, four years older than I, visited the Mississippi Delta, something I was unaware of at the time. But in the mid 1990's, I served as principal of all black, Black Bayou Elementary School in Glendora, Mississippi. Glendora was a major site in Emmett's abduction, torture, and murder, but I had no knowledge of the dark history of Glendora's past when I was principal there and unfortunately, missed a golden opportunity to find out more about the case as the community's trusted principal.

The significance of this small predominately black Delta town being unbeknownst to me in these years, was perhaps ordained by Someone higher—the time not yet right!

Not until February 2017, did I find out the significance of Glendora. This happened while I was writing a screenplay based on my novel *The Gully Path* in which Emmett played a significant role. Then like so many others before me, I began immersing myself in Till research, now limited by the death of most of the primary characters in the real life tragedy. I am no longer trusted as the town's principal and it is harder to get people to open up to me. The best I can do is keep vigil at the main sites in the Till lynching and this is where the extraordinary events began to play out.

On February 26, 2017, my Georgia friends Belinda and Frank rode with me to Sumner, Mississippi, my first visit to the Emmett Till sites. First stop—Sumner Courthouse where we met Bill Foster, a volunteer with the Emmett Till Interpretive Center, who took us through the courthouse which was otherwise locked since it was Sunday. It was Bill who informed us about the Emmett Till Historical Intrepid Center at Glendora a few miles down the road. This was the first I learned of the importance of Glendora in my new quest.

But later when we arrived at Glendora, we found the museum also closed since it was Sunday. In front of the museum, a large agricultural building, a Quonset hut, was wide open, and the hut looked to be as old as the cotton gin now transformed into the museum.

I spent time in the Quonset hut that also shared ground with the now vacant lot where murderer J.W. Milam's house once stood. *(The Quonset hut was completely enclosed less than three months later; my coming in February perfect timing—no coincidence)*! While in the Quonset hut, I began to fill in the timeline with what I believe details the sequence of events on the fateful night and early morning August 27-28, 1955. I realize the events can only be known for sure by those present when the horrendous crime took place—those now dead. So if they are all dead, how did I gain this information? Simply put... EMMETT TOLD ME!

Interior of Sumner Courthouse, restored to exactly the way it was in 1955

Sumner, MS Courthouse: J.W. Milam and Roy Bryant were found not guilty here for the murder of Emmett Till, September 1955. Three months later Milam and Bryant confessed to the murder to journalist William B. Huie for $4000. The courthouse was placed on the National Register of Historic Places in 2010, and in 2014, renovation was completed putting the courthouse back as it was in 1955.

Part I

The Lynching of a Fun-Loving Boy

Chapter One

"Voices"

"Emmett, are you here?"

This is the way I started my first and all subsequent visits to the main sites making up the Emmett Till Memory Project (ETMP) in the Mississippi Delta *(See appendix for information on ETMP)*. To experience the sites is to follow Emmett's last week on earth as a carefree, funny, and impulsive fourteen-year-old boy from Chicago. But I did not know about ETMP when I made my way to the Delta on February 26, 2017. And I had no idea what lay in store, the unplanned activity not deemed possible; nor could it be replicated. As always, I followed the steppingstones placed in my path.

I was meant to begin this journey at Sumner Courthouse even though it is one site Emmett never visited—until recently *(story to follow later)*. But it was at the Emmett Till Interpretive Center across from the Sumner Courthouse where our tour guide Bill Foster gave us a quick summary of the other sites important to Emmett's story.

Just 12.5 miles south of Sumner on Highway 49 lies the small town of Glendora, home to the Emmett Till Historic and Intrepid Center. This museum is full of Emmett Till memorabilia and information about the young boy's tragic murder. Beside and to the front of the Intrepid Center in a now vacant lot is the site where murderer J.W. Milam's house once stood. Across the tracks from the Intrepid Center and at the edge of Glendora lies Black Bayou Bridge, a peaceful scene with a gruesome past—the location where many believe Emmett Till's body was dumped by his murderers into the muddy, snake-infested waters of Black Bayou.

Next stop—Money, Mississippi where the Emmett Till tragedy began with a wolf whistle. After traveling south of Glendora on Hwy. 49, turn east on Hwy. 8, and then south on Money Road for three more miles. Watch on the right for the ruins of Bryant's Store—vine covered in the summer and barely visible through its lush green camouflage. All that is left of the old town of Money is a gas station (closed), and the walls of Bryant's Store now crumbling away into nothingness. Not far away, on Dark Ferry Road is the community of East Money where the home of plantation owner Grover Frederick and the East Money Church of God in Christ with its cemetery can be found.

Retrace the route back to Hwy 8 and continue west to Ruleville. Here, turn north on Hwy 3 and continue to Drew. On the outskirts of Drew, turn left on Drew Ruleville Rd. and follow the road to a beautiful white plantation home on the right with a driveway crossing a pristine bayou filled with ageless cypress knees. Up a slight incline at the end of the driveway, sits a long rustic wooden seed barn that served as a torture chamber for Emmett Till in 1955. Now the barn stands surrounded by beautiful Delta landscape, painstakingly cared for by a well-respected, loving Delta family.

NOTE: For best routes to these and other Emmett Till sites, check out Emmett Till Memory Project (ETMP) for GPS, directions, and a historical description of each site, or visit the website at tillmemoryproject.com.

When my friends and I embarked on this Sunday afternoon ride in February 2017, we had no idea what lay waiting for us. No, I am not new to paranormal happenings! For the last few years, "voices" from the past have found me. *(I have written books in many genres including paranormal mysteries, fiction, and nonfiction).* Since I have a Masters Degree in history and taught it for many years, I am also a history buff and have targeted mostly historical locations in my unusual pastime. Locations I have investigated include historical buildings, homes, hospitals, hotels, ghost towns, schools, cemeteries, and even prisons and insane asylums all over the United States including Alaska, Montana, Colorado, California, Idaho, West Virginia, North Carolina, Tennessee, Kentucky, Arkansas, Louisiana, and Mississippi. I have recorded many EVP's, electronic voice phenomenon or voices recorded on electronic equipment but not often heard by ear, and I have taken pictures of unexplained entities. But it is the "voices" I consider the real evidence and these recorded voices keep me searching and going back to sites.

Because of these investigative efforts and my interest in history, in 2015, I was cast in the A & E five-part series for television *Cursed: The Bell Witch*. Many nights I stood vigil at the graves of Betsy Bell Powell and other Bell family ancestors. Betsy and her family were important characters in the Tennessee legend from the early 1800's, but moved to Yalobusha and Panola Counties in the mid to late 1800's, bringing with them the legend they were unable to keep secret. This secured the legend's place in Mississippi's history as well. Betsy's grave is conveniently located a few miles down the road from my home.

During the filming for the series, I was introduced to spiritual messenger Angel Leigh, and the result was my first attempt at writing nonfiction. *Through the Eyes of Angel Leigh*, also published by Double Dragon Publishing, tells about the life of this intriguing young woman.

I did not go to the Delta in February 2017 to try to catch Emmett's voice even though I always keep myself open to possibilities. I went to learn more about this young boy's ordeal in order to make sure I got his story right in the screenplay I was writing. So much is still not known about what happened in the early hours of August 28, 1955, and I have no misgivings about thinking I will be able to "fill in the gaps" using the same methodology I used, and still use, with Betsy Bell Powell and other historical figures. I realize the nonfiction I am writing comes with no guaranty or proof, other than video footage filmed at the sites. I have every SDHC card I have ever used in videoing just in case I need proof of reported findings. But, ultimately, it is up to each reader to believe or not. As Keith Beauchamp once reminded me, "You know, Sue, there is so much history in these sites, you can never know for sure whose voice you're recording."

My first trip to the Emmett Till sites proved to be an insatiable appetizer necessitating many more trips. With each subsequent visit,

I have picked up new insights into Emmett's personality, character, and some on his fate. Keep in mind, Emmett Louis Till was a young Christian who loved his family, demonstrated care for all those around him, enjoyed going to church, and as such, his soul is now in heaven with his mother Mamie, grandmother Alma, Uncle Mose, Aunt Elizabeth, and many of his family members and friends who now include Emmett's cousin Simeon Wright who passed away on September 4, 2017. As Christians, we have the promise from our Heavenly Father of an afterlife free of pain and sorrow, surrounded by joy, peace, and beauty unimaginable on earth. Any voices caught symbolizing pain and suffering experienced on earth could only be residual, energy left over to replay itself like a broken record giving insight into what happened at the time it occurred but events never remembered or replicated by those hurt when alive but who are now passed. Emmett has passed on and is now with Jesus. He can no longer remember or repeat the pain and suffering of August 28, 1955.

Yes, some "voices" and "sounds" are disturbing, but each time one of these was recorded, I found a positive sign left by Emmett, or possibly by one of God's angels—something up for speculation and theory. Many times I caught and recorded what I believe to be Emmett's chuckles, each one bringing a smile to my face as I listened back on my computer.

Knowing now what a jovial young man Emmett was, I can understand why I recorded him chuckling so many times as I videoed at these sites. And after reading Mamie's *Death of Innocence*, in which she tells how Emmett loved "knock, knock" jokes, I know why I always get three knocks at the seed barn, my most visited site, when I ask, "Emmett, are you here?"

But the sign I found over and over that brought me the greatest peace of mind and comfort were white feathers. In my blessed life of seventy-two years, I have never found a white feather, but after starting my Emmett journey five months ago, four white feathers have been placed in my path, each one at an important Emmett Till site with two feathers at one site. Coincidence? Perhaps, one or even two feathers could be considered coincidence but four? NEVER!

White Feathers from Emmett is divided into two parts for clarity. Part I, "Emmett Till: The Lynching of a Child" provides the reader with background information for a better understanding of this young boy, including before he headed to Mississippi to visit family. Emmett, the All American fourteen-year-old, is explored through his fun-loving personality, his wonderful relationship with his mother Mamie, and his impulsiveness which ultimately led to his fate. The crime will also be covered using graphic descriptive narrative and will include the abduction, torture, and murder. The trial and its aftermath will show justice not received.

Part II, "White Feathers" tells in detail how paranormal investigative techniques were used and will give the results in terms of voices recorded and signs left by Emmett with an explanation of each. I feel very blessed to have been able to bring in a psychic from out-of-state, resulting in new disclosures and confirming some facts believed but never proven.

To help with the flow of the text, I will be using terms such as "Emmett's voice", or "Henry Lee Loggins' voice." In reality, I do not know for sure whose voices I have recorded. I only know what I think based on the context in which the voices were recorded. No one knows or can explain who or what these voices are to one hundred percent accuracy. I only know they exist and trust God for my understanding and safety.

As an author, I have a philosophy that works for me in my writing and in every adventure on which life takes me: "Keep an open mind and an open path, and the WAY will find you." As a Christian, I know the WAY is my Heavenly Father, and I trust Him to steer me in the direction He wants me to go. I pray for guidance; I pray for protection; and at the end of the day, I pray thanking God for having rewarded me with both.

As you read, keep your mind and your path open and allow the WAY to lead you to understanding. Believe or not! Your choice!

Chapter Two

"Knock, Knock!"
"Who's There?"
"Emmett!"

"Emmett was a fun-loving prankster—never had a dull day in his life. Full of fun every day—all the time!" Thus began the description Reverend Wheeler Parker gave during a panel discussion at Sumner Courthouse about his cousin Emmett Till. Not only was Wheeler Parker Emmett's cousin, he was Bobo's best friend in Chicago.

Emmett's nickname Bobo, a clown's name, fit the young comedian well. Reverend Wheeler Parker, a retired pastor and barber, told how Bobo loved jokes. "Emmett would even pay friends to tell him jokes."

Bobo's Mississippi cousin Simeon Wright, two years younger than Bobo, told in his book, *Simeon's Story,* how excited he was Bobo was coming to visit during that fateful August 1955. Simeon knew Bobo would be the center of attention but Simeon also knew he would have Bobo all to himself much of the time, especially at night since they would share a bed.

Simeon went on to tell how he and his brothers did not know Bobo's name was Emmett until after he died. During Wheeler and Emmett's visit, Bobo and Simeon slept together in the room behind Simeon's parents Mose and Elizabeth Wright, in their large six room sharecropper's house in East Money in the Mississippi Delta.

Bobo kept Simeon up all night his first night, telling him stories about life in Chicago. Living up to his showmanship reputation, Bobo dazzled Simeon with tales of Lincoln Park with its many rides, swimming, and all kinds of fun. Then there was Emmett's favorite pastime baseball which often caused him to be late when running errands for his mom. On one occasion, he returned home with a loaf of bread his mom said "looked like it had been used for second base." But it was not just the description of city life that held Simeon's attention.

"I enjoyed the sound of his voice; when Bobo talked, he stuttered, and more so when he got excited, but he used that to capture your attention." Simeon goes on to tell about falling asleep the first night of Bobo's visit, dreaming of playing in the park with Bobo and his friends. Simeon would soon know Lincoln Park and Chicago firsthand, but it would be without his beloved cousin.

In her book *Death of Innocence*, Mamie Till Mobley described the happiness and love surrounding her only child Bo. She told about him running across the alley to his great Uncle Emmett's house to get him to tell him a new joke. Then Bo would run back across to tell his mom the same joke, putting inflections in perfectly for the punch line just as Uncle Emmett had done.

"I heard more chickens crossing more roads, and knock-knock this and knock-knock that." Mamie added how Bo shared riddles, jokes, and some made-up senseless jokes, but even these made the people around him laugh. Even at just six years of age, Bo kept everyone around him laughing.

As Emmett grew older, the jokes made more sense, and he turned from telling jokes to playing jokes on his friends and cousins. In *Death of Innocence*, Mamie recounted one practical joke Emmett played on his friend and favorite joke teller, as well as joke seller, Donny Lee. During the great migration between World War I and World War II, many African-American Mississippians moved from Mississippi to Illinois searching for a better life, and Donny Lee's family had been part of this migration.

Donny Lee was quite a storyteller, priding himself in performing jokes and stories, all long narrative, rhyming tales. Emmett would pay upwards to a dollar for these long jokes. Emmett felt a special relationship with Donny Lee, or T. Jones, as Emmett nicknamed him, because like Emmett, T. Jones stuttered, something causing the boys to laugh at each other when they got their tongues tied up in syllabic run-ons that seemed to go on forever. Mamie told about one time when the boys got stuck ordering at the corner store. Donny Lee's order could not get pass "p-p-p-p-pop" and Emmett could not get past "m-m-m-m-moon pie." The twosome repeated their orders over and over as the joke of the day—but on purpose these times.

Emmett also played practical jokes on his friends. Coming home from a trip to the beach, T. Jones and Emmett decided to carry their clothes and ride home in their swimming trunks. T. Jones went to sleep on the ride home, and when he woke up, he found he was wearing his underwear on his head.

Before Wheeler and another cousin moved to Chicago, they visited Emmett there. Once when walking down 63rd Street, they ran into a tough looking group of boys. Emmett knew his Mississippi country cousins were scared so when they got right beside the thuggish boys, Emmett turned to his cousins and loudly asked, "You say you could beat their what?" The cousins took off running with Emmett laughing all the way while trying to keep up with his faster cousins. On one of many TV specials on Emmett, a former classmate told how one day in gym class, Emmett pulled his shirt up. Emmett, always chubby, began doing a belly roll while his classmates looked on rolling in laughter.

Even in Mississippi on this fateful last trip, Emmett was a comedian with a ready made audience, with laughter pouring from his cousins as Emmett increased his playfulness. Emmett was impressed with the bravery of his cousins who had to "run the snakes" out of the muddy water before they could swim in the lake near their house, but Bobo found a way to pull a prank on them. When they weren't looking, he threw a big log in the water and excitedly told his cousins it was a big old fish.

On Sunday, the day after Emmett's arrival, Maurice, oldest son of Uncle Mose and Aunt Elizabeth Wright, drove the boys to Money to buy fireworks, Emmett's idea. Before the cousins had time to tell Bobo it was against the law to shoot off fireworks in the town limits, the impulsive teen had firecrackers going off in the street.

According to Mamie, every aspect of Bo's daily life was an

opportunity to perform, whether it was repeating with flare, lines from his favorite movies, or doo-wopping with his friends under streetlights used as their own private stage. And, if this was not enough, there was Emmett's comedy act, repeating jokes he had paid for and practiced to perfection. Of course, the jokes always included exaggerated stuttering—something good for bigger laughs. Simeon wrote how he always thought if Bobo had lived, he could have been a comedian like George Gobel, one of Emmett's favorite comedians and someone he often mimicked, performing Gobel's most popular routines.

Mamie wrote in her book:

> For Emmett, life was laughter and laughter was life-giving. There was so much joy in his carefree world that he just wanted to share with everyone around him. He did it the only way a young boy knows how to do it. He made people laugh.

In August of 1955, Emmett's Uncle Mose Wright rode the train to Chicago for a family funeral. When it was time to leave, Mose's grandson Wheeler Parker decided to return with his grandfather to Mississippi for a two-week stay. Immediately, Emmett wanted to go to Mississippi, too, and he carried on so begging and pleading, his mom finally gave in even though she had misgivings about Emmett going to Mississippi. But her boy was a teenager now, and she knew she had to give him the independence to travel with his Uncle Mose and cousin Wheeler.

Knowing Emmett always wanted to look his best, especially in front of his Mississippi cousins he had not seen in years, Mamie took Emmett shopping for new clothes and black penny loafers with crepe soles, his favorite. Then it was off to a flea market to purchase a new wallet, something he needed for the extra spending money he would carry. But it could not be just any wallet.

No wallet was complete without a stock photo of one of Bobo's favorite movie stars. Bobo had a hard time choosing between

Hedy Lamarr and Dorothy Lamour. After going back and forth, staring at the two beautiful white actresses, Emmett decided on Hedy Lamarr, a dark-haired Hollywood star considered to be the most beautiful woman in the world in the 1940's and 50's. Perhaps what took Emmett so long deciding was his daydreaming of stories he would make up to tell his Delta cousins about the beautiful girl whose picture he carried. Emmett could never know what chain of events this picture would set in motion, events with an ending so horrible, it defied anyone's worst imagination!

In Mamie's book, she goes into great detail telling how she preached to her son before handing him over to Uncle Mose. Mamie talked to Emmett about the differences in Chicago and Mississippi for an African American boy. Even though Chicago was segregated, it was a safe haven compared to the Deep South. Emmett was heading into dangerous territory with the state's racist Jim Crow society, a society in which lynching was once viewed as public entertainment. Mamie presented to her son many extreme scenarios he found impossible to believe. After all, Bobo was loved everywhere he went in Illinois; he got along well with kids at his school, was a devoted son and grandson, loved attending church on Sundays, and made himself a helper to the milkman, the iceman, and others, helping with deliveries in his neighborhood. How could Mississippi be that different?

When Mamie told Bobo he would be expected to get off the sidewalk for white women to pass and would have to "humble" himself, even "getting down on his knees" and begging if confronted by angry white men, Bobo replied, "Oh, Mama, it can't be that bad." If one thing was drilled into his head more than any of the other rules of Mississippi white society, it was the importance of saying "sir" and "ma-am" with eyes lowered in an obsequious manner. The more Mamie preached, the more Emmett assured her he knew how to act in Mississippi. He just did not want to believe how bad Mississippi could be. Mamie explained her frustration and fears in one statement: "How do you give a crash course in hatred to a boy who has only known love?"

August 20th finally arrived for the excited teen but it seemed to be taking far too long to get to the train station where Uncle Moses and Wheeler impatiently waited. Was it fate that day that made Mamie call Bo back from the platform he had run to in fear of missing the City of New Orleans train? If only they had been five minutes later, Bo would have missed the train that carried him south to his fate.

"Bo, you didn't kiss me good-bye. How do I know I'll ever see you again?" Mamie called to her son, urging him to take an extra second and run back to her.

"Aw, Mama," Emmett answered but as extra assurance, he not only kissed his mother but handed her his watch saying he would not need it in Mississippi.

"What about your dad's ring?" The day before Emmett was to leave for Mississippi, Mamie had given in and allowed Bo to wear the silver ring left by his dad Louis after his death in 1945. The signet ring carved with initials L.T. for Louis Till would later become an object for identifying Emmett's body—and a mystery. Bo did not give his dad's ring to his mom that day, telling her he wanted to wear the ring to show it off to his cousins in Mississippi.

Mamie took her own watch off and put on her son's watch. Bobo was right. Time was about to come to a standstill for Emmett and his mother. This would be Mamie's last kiss from her son, the handsome boy with hazel eyes, a comedian's stutter leftover from polio he had otherwise conquered when he was a young child, and a contagious smile and chuckle—the son who had made her and his world laugh. And it would be the last time she would see the silver signet ring engraved with initials L.T. proudly worn on Bobo's finger. Soon the ring would mysteriously disappear—forever.

Watch YouTube video: https://youtu.be/RyJO4iTCFn4 titled "A Fun-Loving Emmett!"

Chapter Three

The Wolf Whistle

The sixteen-hour train ride from Chicago was an endurance test for Emmett who could not contain his excitement. Uncle Mose had trouble keeping Emmett in his seat during the long trip, and at one point, Emmett even lost his shoes. Mose and Elizabeth Wright's oldest son Maurice picked the group up at the station in Winona, and Emmett's anticipation grew the closer he got to East Money and the cousins he had not seen in years. Finally, Maurice turned the old Ford on to Dark Ferry Road, the road local blacks called Dark Fear Road for many reasons including tales of lynching and terrorizing blacks by enraged whites. The name would prove especially appropriate by the end of Bobo's and Wheeler's first week in Mississippi.

One of the things Emmett wanted to experience most in Mississippi was picking cotton. After all, how hard could it be pulling white fluff out of hard, prickly bolls and filling a cotton-sack? And to get paid for this would give him even more spending money in Mississippi, not that he needed it. Being an only child of an only child meant being spoiled by not only his mama but also by his grandmother Alma. Emmett seemed to always have a pocketful of change, and traveling to Mississippi meant his mom made sure he had extra.

Come Monday morning, Emmett got the experience he wanted when the first day of cotton picking began. Simeon knew Emmett would be in for a not so joyous surprise. Simeon's dad was a sharecropper and the family depended on this crop to get them through the next year. Simeon knew well the hard work involved in filling a cotton sack. He had been picking cotton since he was just a young child.

Emmett did not come to Mississippi with clothes for cotton picking. While his cousins wore overalls to the field, Emmett went dressed for a party, or church, in nice khaki pants, a shiny shirt, and his black penny loafers. When the nine-foot cotton sack was slung over Emmett's head and across his chest, he realized the heaviness could be a problem. After dragging the sack over a few rows, Emmett barely had enough cotton in it to make a bump and he was drenched in sweat. At the end of the day, Emmett told his Aunt Elizabeth he could not take the heat. She put the word in Mose's ear and Emmett's cotton picking career ended.

Emmett stayed around the house with his aunt and helped her with chores, something he was accustomed to doing for his mom in Chicago. Once he had even baked a cake, another funny Bobo story to be told over and over by his mama. The recipe had called for baking powder but he only had baking soda. Deciding it had to do the same thing, Emmett used the soda only to discover the cake never rose in the oven. Mamie tried to eat the cake but ended up thanking her son for the sweet gesture and laughing as she told the story to her mother Alma and her boyfriend Gene Mobley.

Emmett waited every day for his cousins to come from the field. Cotton picking may not have turned out to be entertaining but swimming in the snake-infested waterhole across the road had proved to be great fun. Even more exciting was stealing watermelons and eating the heart out of them, or running to the store for fireworks which could be bought anywhere in the Delta.

Wednesday night meant church for the Wright family especially since Mose Wright was a part-time minister. But this Wednesday, Mose decided to let the boys off so they could go to the store. He knew they had worked hard picking cotton and needed some free time. Maurice loaded the group into his dad's '46 Ford and off they went.

About 8:00 p.m., the group arrived in Money, Mississippi with Maurice behind the wheel. Maurice (16) did not have a driver's license and had been instructed by Mose to go only to the local store, a small store close to their house, and not to get on the main road to Money. In the car with Maurice were his Chicago nephew Wheeler

Parker (16), brother Simeon Wright (12), brother Robert (14), Wheeler's cousin Pete Parker, Emmett, and two teenage neighbors Roosevelt Crawford and Ruthie Crawford, although in Simeon's book, he insisted no girl was in the car with them.

Elizabeth Wright had warned her sons against taking Bobo to Money because people might not understand him and his city ways or his gregarious personality, and she counted on Maurice and the older boys to keep Bobo from doing "anything stupid." Maurice and the group did not obey Mose and Elizabeth and headed to Money anyway, hoping to make it to a café before it closed. When the group arrived, they found the café closed for the night but they also saw a group of young people playing checkers in front of Bryant's Grocery and Meat Market and decided to join them.

Scenarios conflict at this point, but one young witness reported Bobo showed the wallet photo of Hedy Lamarr to the group and bragged about dating white girls in Chicago. One of the older boys in the group told Emmett he should go inside the store and look at the pretty lady behind the counter. True to his nature, Emmett took the dare and entered the store where he walked to the counter and asked for two cents worth of bubble gum.

In a telephone interview with filmmaker Keith Beauchamp, Keith explained how Emmett loved movies and entertained his friends by imitating scenes from his favorite movies. His favorite actress was Hedy Lamarr, and he carried a photo of her in his wallet, the stock photograph that came in the wallet he had purchased before the trip to Mississippi.

"Hedy Lamarr and Carolyn Bryant almost looked identical." Keith felt this could have been Emmett's thinking. Perhaps this primed boyish acting out or flirtatious looks from Emmett which might have sent up alarm signals to Carolyn. With Emmett's background, he possibly appeared too comfortable in this white woman's presence, something taboo in Mississippi society, but this will never be known for sure since Emmett was in the store alone for a short period of time.

"Nobody else looked like Hedy Lamarr in that area," Keith continued. As fate would have it, Emmett "just happened to stumble across this small country store where this beautiful white woman was behind the counter."

However, the window of time in the store, according to Simeon and other witnesses, did not allow for the aggressive behavior by Emmett described by Carolyn Bryant to the court (without the jury present) during the trial of husband Roy Bryant and his half-brother J.W. Milam. According to Simeon Wright's account, Bobo was in Bryant's store alone with Carolyn Bryant no more than a minute, certainly not enough time to grab her by the waist and ask her for a date, along with making obscene comments about having "been with white girls before."

Two reports are accepted as true happenings. One other report is interesting, to say the least, and could be true but only has one witness. The first report stated when Emmett left the store, he said "goodbye" or "bye bye" to Carolyn Bryant, something unacceptable in the South and considered as acting too familiar with a white woman, especially without showing proper respect and not using "ma'am" after it. Something triggered Carolyn to go to her sister-in-law Juanita Milam's car to retrieve the .38 caliber pistol from under the seat, but it is unknown at the present time exactly what that trigger was unless it was Emmett's too personal "Bye Bye".

Years after the incident, the Wright's neighbor Ruthie Mae Crawford told how she was watching through the window of the store where the checkers were set up and witnessed unacceptable behavior for that time. When Emmett paid for the bubble gum, he placed the money directly in Carolyn Bryant's hand, a "skin-to-skin" gesture not allowed between the two races. Carolyn, supposedly, jerked her hand back to show her distaste for the act by Till. None of the others present witnessed this, or did not report it.

Other than saying "Goodbye", one more reported action by Emmett is known to be true, giving the incident the common title "The Wolf Whistle." As Carolyn came out of the store behind Emmett and Simeon, Emmett stopped and gave a wolf whistle. Saying "goodbye" without the addition of "ma'am" and placing money directly in Carolyn's hand were both against the mores of Mississippi society and would have been construed as "disrespectful" by most whites. The wolf whistle, however, carried sexual innuendoes, especially with the lies Carolyn Bryant would add to the incident in order to defend her husband and his brother during their trial. But for Emmett, his behavior was nothing more than the antics of a silly, impulsive fourteen-year-old boy and were consistent with his personality. Even his uncle had heard him whistle at pretty girls that week.

Emmett's wolf whistle triggered alarm in all of those with him. Emmett realized too late what he had had done, and his fear showed as he scurried after his group running to Uncle Mose's old Ford, piling in with the others, and speeding away from the store.

As Maurice drove the group down the isolated, dark country roads, he saw headlights coming fast behind him, and he was sure someone was following them. Quickly, he pulled over, and the group, all but young Simeon who hid in the floorboard, ran into a cotton field to hide. The car passed on by and the young people laughed at their unfounded fear as they returned to the car. At Emmett's pleading, they all agreed not to tell Mose and Elizabeth. However, both parents found out about it, most likely from a Crawford neighbor who also lived on the Grover Frederick Plantation.

In 2010, Carolyn Bryant gave an interview with historian and author Timothy B. Tyson. This was the first interview she had granted since Emmett's murder. In Tyson's book *The Blood of Emmett Till*, released in 2017, Carolyn Bryant admitted to what most already believed: the physical advances made by Emmett Till in Bryant Store, the ones she testified to in court in 1955, were prefabricated lies. The world will probably never know exactly what Carolyn Bryant remembers about the Till murder or what happened at that store —at least not until a specified time in the future. Carolyn gave Tyson a copy of her memoirs to be archived and used in the future by research scholars. Her "coming clean" in 2010 was best summarized in Carolyn's statement to Tyson, something Emmett's mother Mamie knew even better than Carolyn Bryant: "Nothing that boy did could ever justify what happened to him."

Old Money from the 1950's
(Photographs Courtesy of Mike Turner)

Bryant Grocery and Meat Market in Money, MS in 1955, was the scene of the "Wolf Whistle" incident, the beginning of the end for Emmett Till. Emmett whistled at Carolyn Bryant, a pretty young woman working in the store owned by her husband Roy. The whistle ultimately led to Emmett's abduction, torture, and murder three days later. Roy Bryant purchased the store (merchandise and use of building) from C.B. Turner. Only days after selling it to Roy Bryant, Mrs. Turner told her family she had a feeling selling to Roy Bryant had been the wrong thing to do.

Mr. and Mrs. C.B. Turner, original owners of Bryant Store

"Good ole days?"

Life in Mississippi in the 1950's meant two very different things for blacks and whites. "Separate and Unequal" was the way things were and to cross the color lines was to cross into dangerous territory if you were black in Mississippi in the days of Jim Crow.

In 1955, Money consisted of one line of about 4 or 5 stores.

Gas station across from Bryant Store

Railroad Depot in Old Money (now part of the Church Annex Building, behind where the old stores had been located)

"Money was a good place to grow up." Mike Turner (pictured) speaks with pride in his hometown. "I don't want people thinking my family members, neighbors, and friends were all racists and backwoods rednecks. That is just not true."

Money's white school in the 1950's

First grade classroom at Money School, 1950's

In 1954, the year before Emmett's murder, the Supreme Court announced a landmark decision. *Brown vs. the Board of Education of Topeka* declared state laws, establishing separate schools for blacks and whites, unconstitutional. Most southern whites, especially in Mississippi, became fearful of white children and black children going to school together, afraid of "mixing" the races.

Many extremists expressed their outrage through heightened discrimination and violence against African Americans. White Citizens Councils were formed, the first being in Indianola, Mississippi in 1954, and even though they claimed to be opposed to violence against blacks, some were known to have hired the KKK to perform violent acts of intimidation against blacks. A favorite means of keeping blacks under tabs was to take out ads in local newspapers and list the names of any blacks who registered to vote or who joined the NAACP. This meant loss of jobs and income for those persons listed.

In *Simeon's Story*, Simeon Wright talks about going to school at Money Vocational Grade and High School, serving black students first through twelfth grades. Black students were bussed far from their homes to substandard schools, passing nice white schools on the way. Simeon was in the top five in his class at Money but each school year was cut short because of cotton-picking, something not true for most of the white schools. When his father relocated his family to Chicago after Emmett's murder, Simeon who had completed fifth grade, was able to attend school a full school term for the first time in his life. Simeon was also exposed to white teachers for the first time, teachers he found to be helpful and kind. Life in Chicago was different but not harsh like in the Mississippi Delta. He no longer had to work in the cotton fields and could concentrate on his education. Simeon did well in school in Chicago and graduated from high school in 1962.

Even though the court ruled separate schools unconstitutional in 1954, it would be another decade before integration would really begin in Mississippi. In *Silver Rights* written by Constance Curry, the true story is told of the Carter family from Drew, Mississippi in

Sunflower County, adjacent to Leflore County where the Wrights had lived. Mae Bertha and Matthew Carter were tired of their children being educated in substandard black schools. In reality, in the 1950's, black schools in Sunflower County were often just run down one room churches, and students did not start school until November when cotton picking was over. The schools had few supplies and were forced to use old torn textbooks discarded by the white schools. Teachers might have a high school education but most did not.

In 1965, the sharecropping Carter parents, signed papers under the "Freedom of Choice" Plan and enrolled their eight youngest children in Drew Public Schools to give them a better education and secure a future "out of the cotton fields." Mae Bertha and Matthew Carter faced condemnation by whites resulting in economic devastation and increased poverty but they refused to give up. Seven out of their last eight children later graduated from the University of Mississippi.

Chapter Four

The Abduction

Three days passed without incident and Emmett's wolf whistle at Bryant's store was put out of the young boys' minds. On the next Saturday August 27th, Mose took the boys to Greenwood as a treat for their Chicago visitors and for a needed reprieve after a hard first week of cotton picking. His wife Elizabeth stayed home in Money. In Greenwood, Mose visited friends and family while the boys enjoyed their own activities including western movies for Simeon and looking for girls by the teenagers who walked up and down the streets eating and watching the dancing in nightclubs. A late stop by 4/5 Plantation gave the older boys a taste of white lightning but no girl chasing.

The trip to Greenwood was pleasant, and when the group got back to Mose's house, the teens went straight to bed, falling into exhausted sleep. Heavy knocking at the door around 2:30 a.m. startled Mose, Elizabeth, and Wheeler Parker, waking them from their deep sleep.

"Preacher? Preacher? This is Mr. Bryant!"

Preacher knew Mr. Bryant owned the store at Money, and he and Elizabeth feared they knew why the man was at their door. Hurriedly, Elizabeth slipped out of bed and headed for Bobo who was asleep in the room next to theirs. Preacher took his time feeling his way through the dark house taking advantage of extra time needed since no lights worked in the house.

Once Mose opened the door, the bigger man with the baldhead took up the conversation asking Mose about the boy from Chicago. With a .45 caliber pistol in one hand and a flashlight in the other, Milam forcefully told Preacher, "I want the boy that done the talkin' at Money."

Elizabeth had slipped into the boy's bedroom and made her way to the bed where Bobo was sleeping with her youngest son Simeon. She shook Emmett, speaking softly, trying to arouse him from sleep so she could get him out the back door and into the woods to hide. But Emmett, too groggy from the outing, could not be awakened before the men entered the house. Mose led the two men into the other bedrooms first, the ones not occupied by Emmett, probably as a delaying tactic.

"In the South when the moon don't shine, be home before sundown!" Wheeler Parker looked into the faces of the audience full of teachers in the courthouse at Sumner in June 2017, as he recounted his traumatizing experience the night Emmett was abducted. "A man sitting right there *(points to seat)* once said to me, 'I guess you forgot what happened that night.' Forgot? Forgot? How do you forget something that traumatic?"

It is hard to imagine Reverend Parker, now in his seventies, as the same sixteen-year-old boy who rode the train from Chicago with Emmett and experienced the wolf whistle, the abduction, and then attended his cousin's funeral a few days later in Chicago. The audience of teachers hung on Wheeler's every word as he continued:

"I'm hearing the footsteps coming my way; I'm stretching and looking, praying, shaking, and then they walk in—a gun in one hand and a flashlight in the other. Waiting to be shot, I close my eyes."

Wheeler describes the "pure hell" of that fateful night ending for him with the two men leaving his room and heading into Simeon's bedroom where Bobo was still asleep. Wheeler knew what the men wanted and knew the hell would continue into Bobo's room.

"Are you the one that done the smart talk up at Money?" Milam shined the flashlight in Emmett's eyes as he sat on the side of the bed?

"Yeah." Emmett was not fully awake, or perhaps he did not realize the danger in his reply, when he answered, failing to use "sir"—the one rule his mother had pounded into him before heading south. Full of anger, Milam threatened to blow Emmett's head off if he answered him like that again. Milam then ordered Emmett to get dressed and not to waste time putting socks on with his loafers.

"I don't wear shoes without socks." Emmett answered without thinking, causing Milam to lash out at him again.

When Elizabeth pleaded for the men to spare Bobo, even offering them money, Milam ordered her to, "Get back in bed, and I mean, I want to hear the springs!"

Mose tried to convince the men just to "take him outside and whip him" and explained Emmett had polio as a young child and didn't "have good sense." His attempts to prevent them from taking his nephew failed.

"How old are you?" Milam asked Mose before leaving. When Mose answered he was sixty-four, Milam warned him he would never see sixty-five if he identified him or his brother or told what they did this night.

Mose followed the men out with Emmett but stopped on the porch in the pitch black dark of night, not able to see them once the flashlight was turned off. Mose told during the trial how he heard the men ask someone in the vehicle, someone with a "voice softer than a man's", if Emmett was the one. She replied "yes", and the abductors drove away with Emmett, heading toward Money without even turning on the headlights. The night was so dark, Mose could not tell if it was a car or a pickup the kidnappers were driving.

Elizabeth ran to the nearest white neighbor's house hoping to call the sheriff or someone but the neighbors refused to help her, possibly out of fear for themselves even though they were white. When Elizabeth returned to her house, she was so upset she demanded Mose take her to the house of her brother Crosby Smith in Sumner. Mose did as his wife asked, leaving the boys home alone.

Once his grandparents left, Wheeler told how he got up and put his shoes on so he could run and hide in the woods if the men came back. Shaking in terror, he and Simeon stayed awake until Mose came back after sunrise. They would never see Bobo alive again.

The praying Wheeler Parker did that night as a terrified sixteen-year-old boy, included a promise to God to serve Him if He would just allow Wheeler to make it through the night without being murdered by these unfeeling white men. Years later, Wheeler made good to his end of the bargain and became a minister in Chicago. In 2005, Reverend Wheeler Parker, now beginning his senior years, would conduct a memorial service for his cousin Emmett Till as he was laid to rest a second time after his body was exhumed by the FBI for an autopsy.

Grover Frederick Home on Dark "Fear" Road, East Money

Grover Frederick, plantation owner whose land Mose Wright farmed as a sharecropper, owned the house (see pictured) closest to Mose and Elizabeth Wright. Elizabeth ran to another neighbor's house after the kidnappers left with Emmett but the white neighbors would not help her. The wife wanted to help but the husband would not, probably out of fear for his family.

Even though Mose Wright got along well with plantation owner Grover Frederick, Elizabeth would probably have gotten the same reaction had she run to his door the night Emmett was kidnapped. After Mamie found out her son had been kidnapped, she called the Fredericks but Grover Frederick offered her only excuses of why he could not help her such as not being able to hear on the phone and not having a pencil or paper to write down what she was saying. The truth was most whites feared men like J.W. Milam and Roy Bryant and would not think of crossing them.

Chapter Five

The Lynching

What thoughts filled Emmett's mind the night he was carted away from his great uncle's sanctuary? One thing is assured even without witness or participant testimony. Emmett was terrified!

Many questions remain not fully answered about that night: What was the sequence of events leading up to Emmett's death? Who were the accomplices, blacks and whites? Where did Emmett take his last breath? Where did the murderers dump Emmett's body?

I trust the historians, researchers, and authors listed in the "Works Consulted" section in the Appendix to be credible and as complete in their research as they could possibly be given the many conflicting stories. Considering the brutality of the crime, any information detailed in this chapter must be swallowed in incremental doses, something necessary to prevent the reader/researcher/writer from becoming emotionally overtaxed—or from going insane!

WARNING! The following is brutal and graphic just as the crime committed against Emmett Till. Is it fiction or nonfiction? Answer: Both—but it will never be known for sure how much of each. The information describing acts of cruelty was told to be believed at some point, either by J.W. Milam and/or Roy Bryant in personal interviews, in the article in *Look Magazine*, or by a witness or an accomplice to the crime. The following narrative is no more grotesque than what we know happened to Emmett based on the FBI autopsy report from 2005, on witness accounts, and on interviews conducted with Milam and Bryant. Some information was surmised from voices and words recorded on video camera in specific locations, information gained through paranormal means.

What is known without a doubt is a young boy, barely fourteen-years-old, suffered tremendously in his last few hours on earth; he was dreadfully tortured and murdered and his murderers went free. J.W. Milam and Roy Bryant, as well as others not named at the time, were heartless, despicable, cruel men who lacked morality and human decency. Their crime committed against this young boy was unconscionable.

Two interviews proved crucial in filling in the timeline of events that fateful early morning August 28, 1955. As part of Bonnie Blue's extensive personal investigation into the Till case in 1977, she conducted three telephone interviews with J.W. Milam who mistook her, as she quoted in her book, for "a friendly young white girl." Blue used narrative novel form to present her research in *Emmett Till's Secret Witness: FBI Confidential Source Speaks*.

In the second interview in 1985, Roy Bryant allowed a friend, who wished to remain anonymous, to tape a conversation in which he (Roy) gave, not only new information about his involvement in the lynching of Emmett Till, but Roy guided the friend to sites of Emmett's torture and murder. Roy, like his brother J.W., refused to name other participants in the abduction, torture, and murder telling his friend he was the only one who knew and the information would go to the grave with him.

One thing is certain from both of these interviews. Neither Roy Bryant, nor J.W. Milam showed any remorse for what they had done. Milam died in 1977 of cancer, and Bryant died in 1995 of cancer. Their only concern was for their own well-being.

With all of this in mind, the following narrative is NOT farfetched!

NOTE: The following is a partially fictionalized account written by Jeff Gentry but with historical accuracy and based on accepted research, FBI Autopsy Report from 2005, Trial Transcript of Milam and Bryant Trial, and paranormal events videoed and recorded by Dr. Sue Clifton at important Emmett Till sites in the Mississippi Delta in Leflore County, Tallahatchie County, and Sunflower County.

I can hardly breathe! Dust is all over me.

Emmett cups his swollen eye with his hand, wishing he had some ice from the iceman in Chicago, the one he always helped with deliveries.

My eye hurts so bad! My body feels like I been run over by the City of New Orleans.

Emmett brushes at his shirt and wants to clean the toe of his new penny loafers by rubbing each one against the back of his pants legs like he always does but he cannot move. Besides, Emmett cannot see his loafers through the thick, dark Delta night, but he knows they are covered in dust just like he is.

The black man the others call Henry Lee Loggins sits in the back of the new pickup with his lower body partially stretched over Emmett's legs restraining him. The sweaty man has a familiar odor reminding Emmett of Uncle Moses after a day of picking cotton in the heat. The boy shakes his head remembering, tears welling behind his eye sockets as he longs for the love and attention he has felt from his auntie and uncle this past week.

Where they takin' me? He tries to move but can only wiggle the toes on one foot.

This man too heavy on me! He gon' break my legs if we don't stop soon!

When Emmett talks in his head, he does not stutter but when he is excited or scared, his stuttering grows worse. Tonight he will try to keep quiet, something he was told to do by Loggins while they were in the big open metal building.

Two grown black men! How come they don't help me? Henry Lee Loggins told me he didn't want to get in trouble with the boss man but that ain't no reason for a grownup not to help a kid. I don't know about the other one they call Two Tight Collins.

Emmett leans his head back against the bumpy cab, keeping his thoughts to himself, not wanting to open his mouth and catch even more dust as it forms a cloud behind the moving truck. His thoughts turn to his mama and home.

If I ever get back to Chicago, I'm not ever leaving Mama again! Mississippi ain't on my vacation list anymore!

Emmett raises his hand to his face, brushing the dust from his eyes, mouth, and hair. He knows he's passing cotton field after cotton field even if he can't see them. The sickening odor burns his nostrils and lodges in his throat. He first smelled the awful scent in Uncle Mose's backyard, cut short with the need to use every inch for cotton planting. The smell is like nothing Bobo has ever smelled in Chicago, something unique to the cotton land and used to kill an insect called a boll weevil, or so Simeon told him when he asked what the bad smell was. Simeon had showed him sacks full of the white powder stored in the shed out back.

Bile traces its way from the pit of Bobo's stomach like a toxic volcano and makes its way to his throat threatening to spew. The boy swallows hard trying not to puke as nausea wells up again from swallowing so much dust—so much fear.

Cotton poison!

The poison and dust make him blow snot from his nose which he wipes with the back of his arm and then onto his shirt. Sweat pours down his face and neck and mixes with dust and nose drippings forming droplets of slime on his once nice shirt. Emmett cannot see his clothes in the dark but knows he is dirtier than he has ever been, even dirtier than when he plays baseball in the park.

Sharp dresser! That's what Simeon had noticed about him that day he got out of the car smiling at his cousins. They were all waiting on the porch ready to greet him. But here in the back of this truck, tearing down dusty Delta roads, Emmett does not feel like a sharp dresser.

"Where we g-g-g-oin'?" Emmett finally gets up the courage to ask the man holding his legs but the man says nothing. The two black men remain quiet. Emmett knows there are four white men in the cab including the big baldheaded man with the gun and flashlight and the shorter, quieter man who Uncle Mose called Mr. Bryant. Uncle Mose had begged the big man just to "whip the boy and let him go." The man told his uncle they would "bring him back and put him in the bed" if he was not the right one. Emmett wished he had not told the big man he was "the one that did the talk at Money" when he was getting dressed in Uncle Mose's house. But then, they might have taken Wheeler or Curtis since they said they were looking for the Chicago boy.

Emmett stares into the darkness—all thoughts muted. Then the night replays itself, not just in Emmett's head, but in the mind of the man who holds him captive in the back of the truck.

At first Emmett was thrown in the backseat of a car between the two black men. Up front, the pretty lady from the store, the one who looked like Hedy Lamarr, sat between the two men who took him from Uncle Mose's house. Emmett saw the woman's face when the man they called Roy flicked his lighter to light her cigarette. The two men in the front seat took turns drinking from a jar of white lightning, something they had already had too much of by the smell drifting through the car.

After a short ride, the big man pulled the car in front of a brick building and the woman got out and headed in through a door at the back where a third man passed her, making his way to the car. As the headlights hit the building, Emmett recognized the Bryant Grocery and Meat Market sign across the front. Now he knew what was happening and terror seized him. Ruthie Mae had said the white folks wouldn't forget his wolf whistle.

After a seemingly endless ride down a paved road, the driver pulls the car into a yard beside a big open metal building. Inside, a new green and white Chevy pickup sits, shining under the lights.

"Cut that g—damn light out in there!" Milam calls to the men standing in the yard. A black man runs to turn the light out. "Henry, get the nigga out of the truck."

Henry lets the tailgate down and prods Emmett to jump to the ground.

Five or six white men flood the scene, coming from every direction, all laughing, cursing, and shining flashlights all around like boys playing spotlight. One of the new men shines his flashlight in Emmett's face causing him to cover his eyes.

"Boy! You in a heap a shit! You know it?"

Emmett peeks at the stranger but says nothing.

"Answer him, you little black son 'uva bitch!" The big man hits Emmett across the face with the flashlight, knocking him to the ground.

Emmett wishes he could show the mean man he's tough but all he can do is bury his face in the dirt and cry like a big old baby.

"I w…w…want Mama! I w…w…w…ant to go home! I ain't did n…n…nothin'!" Emmett turns over and looks up at the man holding the flashlight and covers his face with his hands as the giant of a man moves to stand over him. "P…p…p…lease don't hit me ag…g…g…ain, sir!"

The big man jerks Emmett to his feet and shoves him toward Henry Loggins.

"Throw him in the back of the truck. Too many nosy folks 'round here. We'll finish somewhere else."

"Yessuh." Henry Loggins pulls the boy to the truck and orders him to climb in back. Emmett's nose and mouth are bleeding and he sniffs, his crying changing to short snubs.

"Hush yo'self! Jus' make it worse!" The voice is deep but Emmett can detect some concern from the man's whispers and he hopes the man will help him.

"Two Tight, go to the tool shed and get some rope, an ax, and a shovel." J.W. Milam calls to the younger black man outside the metal building before turning to the group of white men gathered around him.

"Come on in the house and I'll tell y'all what we got planned. I won't need all of you this time. It'll be just like I told you at the last meetin'. I'll help you with anything that keeps a nigga in his place cause can't nobody work a nigga, or work a nigga over like I can." Milam laughs and the others laugh with him. "But when it's a family matter, me and Roy will take care of it without the Klan. But be ready in case we need you later. Let's head in the house now 'fore we leave with the little black bastard. Juanita ain't home, and we gon' be mighty thirsty by the time daylight breaks." Laughing, the rest of the white men follow Milam leaving Emmett with Henry Loggins.

Loggins is perched on the side of the pickup bed, trying not to look at the boy who sits silent at his feet. Through the thick, dark quiet of the Quonset hut, he hears the boy speak softly, obviously afraid Big Milam will hear him.

"Help me! You the one brought me."
Emmett's voice is sing-song, something Loggins probably finds unusual. The black man does not know it but this is Emmett's way of trying not to stutter. His mama insisted Emmett memorize speeches and all kinds of things to help his stuttering, and she always told him to whistle when he got stuck on words. But while doo-wopping under the street lights with his buddies back home, Emmett learned he did not stutter when he sang lyrics. Hoping it will help, Emmett begs for his life like he's singing a song, not wanting his stuttering to get in the way of his pleading.

Loggins sits quiet, not answering for a few seconds.
He jus' a chile! Ain't nothin' but a boy cryin' fo' his mama. Here I am 'bout to have another baby o' ma own. What if 'is was my boy these white bastards were doing this to?
Loggins wipes his brow with his bandana and looks away. Perhaps to ease his own conscious, he answers Emmett.
"I can't…I can't get in trouble…wi' duh boss."

Soon the truck fills again with four white men in the cab and Henry Loggins and Two Tight Collins in the back with Emmett. They ride for what seems like hours passing cotton fields, turning off on dark dirt roads only to load up again when "Big", another name the others call Milam, curses and kicks the dirt before announcing, "This ain't it!"
Sometimes, Milam gets so mad when he can't find the right place, he slaps Emmett across the face like it's his fault.
Soon, dim light can be seen in the horizon.
"Shit, J.W.! 'Daylight comin'!" Roy has grown impatient. "We got to get off the road. You ain't gon' find that high bluff over the river. Let's go to Leslie's place. We can finish in the barn. Les is family. Makes it right fo' him to help."

The Delta is serenely quiet as daylight breaks. The only sound heard is the cicadas chirping to hasten the rising of the sun and to warn of the intensity of the hot August day ahead—and of the hotheads in whose hands lies the fate of Emmett Till. J.W. Milam pulls the pickup on to a long driveway crossing a bayou, a serene sight with cypress knees standing as they have stood for decades, guardians of the black water—but not of Emmett Till.

An older black teenage boy walks beside the road. He turns and watches the pickup as it heads across the bayou.

Emmett sees the boy looking and thinks the boy waves but he isn't sure. Emmett can hardly see, his eye is so badly swollen from Milam's strike with the flashlight, and made even worse by slaps and punches with fists at the extra stops. Milam parks the pickup in front of a long wooden barn.

"Get him outa the truck, Henry, and bring him in the barn." Milam barks his orders and heads to the long seed barn and slides the big middle door open.

Jumping to attention, the two black men snatch Emmett from the back of the truck and drag him kicking and crying toward the barn. Again terror overtakes the boy as he tries to pull away from the strong men but to no avail.

"Get the damn nigga in here! It's gettin' late!" Roy Bryant joins in and then looks toward the house that sits a good piece from the barn. Roy waves at another man walking toward them.

When the man sees Henry and Two Tight dragging a black boy into the shed, he starts cussin'.

"Hell, Roy, I ain't got no time for none of this with damn work calling me!" He shakes his head as he walks faster toward the barn.

J.W. and Roy laugh, ignoring him as they enter the seed barn, pulling the door closed behind them except for a small opening just big enough for the new man to enter. Quickly, the man they call Leslie hurries in, his angry face shows he's not ready to greet company.

"I'm serious, J.W.! Got cotton in the fields ready to be picked. My niggas are waiting on me right now! I don't care if y'all are my brothers, this can wait 'til sundown." Leslie Milam pulls a pack of cigarettes out of J.W.'s shirt pocket and takes one out and puts it between his lips.

"Well, this here is a family matter, Leslie, and last time I checked with Mama, you was part of this here family, the Milam part anyway, so I reckon you're in." J.W. takes the pack from Leslie's hand and puts it back in his front shirt pocket.

Leslie Milam glances at the black boy who is struggling to get free.

"This the one from up north I hear whistled at Carolyn?"

Roy's face shoots red as he swears, turning into a mad man and taking his frustrations out on Emmett who whimpers as Roy Bryant steps toward him. Roy's fists tighten into balls of hate.

"G--D--- it! I guess the whole GD Delta has heard about it, and I just found out yesterday! I'm gonna whip Carolyn's ass agin when I get home 'fo shamin' me like this. Time to pay, nigga boy!"

Roy punches Emmett in the face and then hits him hard in the stomach. Henry and Two Tight try to hold the boy up, but Emmett is heavy as he slumps forward, all 150 pounds of nothing but dead weight.

"Well, hell! Let's get it over with then. Sooner the better!" Leslie Milam moves toward Emmett and slaps him across the face while Henry and Two Tight continue holding the boy in an upright position as he screams and cries out in pain.

"Tie him to that pole. Looks like a whippin' pole to me! How many niggas you killed in here, Leslie?" Roy does not laugh as he pulls the rope out of his back pocket and heads toward a tall wooden pole running from the ceiling to the ground.

Not too many." Leslie takes up the joke. "But you know tha's always room in the Tallahatchie River for mo' niggas! But I usually just go down the road to Whore's Lake to dump 'em. Lots closa!" The group laughs.

"Here tell some of the Klan wives killed a few nigga whores not long ago and even a little girl out this way." Roy lights up a cigarette.

"Yeah. Some of them Klan women some mean bitches when it come to their men and they nigga whores! If I was their men, I'd be 'fraid to go to sleep in the same house. 'Fraid I'd wake up missin' some of my best parts!" The men laugh.

Too Tight pretends not to be listening but he already knows what the men are telling is true. In his mind, he goes over the stories he's been told.

When the Klan wives catch their husbands with black "ho's", they kidnap 'em and beat 'em, killin' the ho when they should be killin' they husband. Den they throw the woman's body in Ho Lake, jes down the road. Some of the Klan beat and kill they black women after they finish with 'em, and I hear tell they even kill some little black girls, maybe cause they daddy is the white man; maybe cause the mean basta'ds doin' the little girls, too.

"Can't say as I agree wi' killing that little nigga gal." Another man speaks up. "She couldn't help it none her white daddy got hung up in her nigga mama like a mongrel dog in heat. Boy, I heard tell that white bitch was one mean woman when she was beatin' that little nigga girl. Wudn't more than four or five years old. Kid kept cryin', 'Mama…help me!' Whole time her mammy jus' layin' on the ground drippin' wi' blood. I reckon that tale was truth."

Emmett's hazel eye, the one not swollen, listens to the men talking and wonders how they could do that to a little girl. J.W. Milam moves toward Emmett and grabs him around the neck putting him in a headlock.

"What you gonna do? What you gonna do?" Emmett cries out.

"You gon' figga it out real quick, boy! Here, Two Tight! Hold his hands up high on this pole. Put him on his tiptoes in them fancy shoes!" The black men stretch the boy's arms as high up the pole as they can reach, lifting Emmet to where his weight stretches him causing his shirt to pull up showing his belly fat. Roy firmly slaps the boy's fat and then slaps his face so his head rolls back and forth. Emmett flails against the pole trying to avoid the hits, but his toes won't even reach the ground.

"Please, sir! I'm s-s-sorry! I didn't mean n-n-n-nothin' by it! I won't do it again!" Emmett cries loud, begging, pleading, but all it does is make the madmen laugh and hit harder.

"Well now, you right 'bout that!" J.W. Milam hits Emmett across the face with the end of his .45 Colt, a strike using a force greater than a hammer. "You figga' out what we gonna do, boy? Fat nigga boy gon' whistle at a white woman!"

The men take turns hitting Emmett with fists and pistols as the boy screams through a mouth full of blood. His head bangs against the pole with each hit.

"Mama, please help me!" He screams but no help comes. "Please, God! Don't do it again!" The answer is harder licks across the already bulging eye. Soon, the eye dislodges and hangs on the boy's cheek to the amusement of the white men. The black men look away.

"Damn nigga oughta be out by now but he jus' keeps hollerin'!" One of the other white men gets several good licks in with a thick leather strap, striking high, leaving gashes on the boy's arms and causing the rope to give way. Emmett slumps to the ground and attempts to crawl but no strength is left in him.

Kicking begins in earnest now, and the boy covers his head with his hands. The men kick hard making contact with the boy's hands fracturing both. The wrists dangle as if never attached. Milam kicks the boy in the stomach hard with his boot and the boy barely groans.

Roy moves away and lights up a cigarette. Then he moves back in and holds the cigarette to the boy's bloody cheek. No yells are audible now, and the black men secretly hope the boy has lost consciousness, or better still, maybe he's dead. But just as they think it is over, Emmett's body twitches and the vile men think he is trying to get away.

"Where the hell you thank you goin'?" One of the men grabs one of Emmett's legs and twirls him on to his back. The heavy men take turns jumping on the boy's upper leg until they hear the crack of the main bone, the femur. Emmett lies still and silent.

"Damn, I'm tired! Beatin' niggas is worsen drivin' a truck! Let's dump him at the hospital and get home." Roy leans against the pole.

"Hospital? Have you lost your mind? This nigga's a dead nigga! Ain't but one place for him and that's the Tallahatchie!" Leslie laughs at Roy's remark and one of the other white men, not a brother to Milam and Bryant, runs out back and throws up.

"I believe he's right, Roy. This here's a dead nigga if I eva seen one!" One of the other men they call Melvin pokes Emmett with the toe of his shoe, a fancy dress shoe like he ought to be going to church.

Emmett lies lifeless and the men, tired from their exertion, light up cigarettes and pass the jar of moonshine. Milam leaves the barn and goes to the well for a drink of water. He notices the black kid he passed earlier walking away from the well carrying a bucket of water.

The teenage boy, does a quick look back and gives a slight nod at Milam but continues walking toward the road, back to the sharecropper's house. Milam pays him no attention as he gulps water, pouring some over his bald head before returning to the torture shed.

As he nears the road, the teenage boy sees other field workers' heads pop up out of cotton rows where they've been hiding and listening to what's going on in the seed barn while keeping low so they can't be seen. The boy heads for his aunt's house and is greeted with her holding the door cracked open for his quick entry. She, too, has been peeking through closed curtains and listening through the raised window. When he gets close enough, she grabs his shirt and pulls him through the crack and closes the door behind him.

"Can't believe what they doin' to whoever in that shed, Willie! It just ain't right! It just ain't right!" The aunt shakes her head in disbelief as she returns to the window.

"It ain't nothin' but a boy, Aunt Amanda! I seen him in the back of the truck when they turn in." Amanda takes her station at another window.

Emmett lies unconscious and dreams. He is in his bedroom

in Chicago under the quilt given to him by his grandmother Alma. He hated the cover, thinking the flowers and leaves too girly when his grandmother gave it to him but he thanked her for it anyway. Now, he hugs it tight under his chin, reveling in its soft security. Without opening his eyes, he feels his mama wrap her arms around him with all the love she can give.

"Bo, time to get up. Wake up, baby! Wake up." Emmett opens his eyes, and is greeted by her sweet smile. He smiles back and mouths the most loving name he knows.

"Mama?"

A bucket of cold water floods Emmett's face, loosening a stream of blood that covers the shed floor. Reality returns! Again, Emmett gets a burst of adrenaline from somewhere inside and yells at his attackers.

While Roy and Milam continue to pound Emmett with their fists, Leslie reaches and picks up the wallet that has fallen out of Emmett's pocket. Leslie opens it, takes out the three dollars and puts it in his pocket. Then he notices two pictures.

"Well, would ya' looky here?" Leslie hands Roy the pictures. One is the picture of Hedy Lamarr and the other is a picture of Emmett's grandmother Alma who looks like a white woman.

"What you doin' with pictures of white women, you lil son uva bitch?" Roy shows the pictures to J.W., and he takes his pistol and bashes Emmett's head in. Blow after blow, Milam dishes out with all the force his big frame allows until the boy's skull splits. Blood and tissue fly all over the shed and the other men jump back. The boy lies without stirring—a stillness signaling death, or it should.

"Look at this damn mess!" Leslie yells. "I'm not cleaning this shit up!"

"My niggas'll do it, Leslie. Don't you worry none."

Milam beckons to the black men who move closer.

"Get his clothes off." Milam orders Loggins and Collins to remove Emmett's bloody clothes and make a pile.

Roy grabs a long pair of sheers from a shelf in the shed and heads for Emmett who lies naked. The others begin cursing, telling him to stop.

"I'm gonna make sure this nigga neva thinks uh _____ a white woman again! He deserves it! No tellin' what he wuz thankin' when he whistled at ma' wife!"

"Shit, man! Can't you see he's dead? No need for that!" Leslie holds on to Roy's arm.

"He's right, Roy. He's done. Let's get rid of him." J.W. takes the sheers from his brother's hand and throws them next to the back wall. It's then J.W. notices the drill and bit lying on a work table.

"Too bad I didn't see that before now. Could have drilled right through the nigga's thick skull and saved messin' up my pistol." Milam wipes his .45 Colt on his pants leg before returning it to his holster.

Milam kicks Emmett in the groin as hard as he can and walks to the door. Emmett does not move.

Milam backs his pickup into the middle of the barn, and motions for Loggins and Collins.

The black men pick the boy up and throw him in the back of the truck, covering him with a tarpaulin Leslie retrieved from the barn.

"Damn, he nasty!" The smaller black man Collins shakes his head and holds his nose as he turns away from the truck.

"I'll take you two and we'll bury his clothes. I've had enough of this. But first y'all clean up the mess on the shed floor. Spread that cottonseed yonda' all over it. Can't have nobody askin' questions." Leslie gives orders to the two black men who are glad not to have to ride on the truck with the body.

Somewhere along the Delta road now filled with bright morning sunlight, Emmett Till lies alone in the back of the pickup truck, the one bought by J.W. Milam three days earlier in Charleston on the same day the young black boy from Chicago whistled at Carolyn Bryant. The boy's battered body lies unmoving under a tarpaulin. But if a car happens to pull up behind the pickup on the road back to Glendora, the driver might back off, noticing red liquid leaking from the truck's bed and splattering onto the pavement as the pickup moves speedily toward the finale.

When J.W. pulls in at Glendora into the empty Quonset hut, he calls two more black men in and gives them orders. One goes to the cotton gin out back and brings back a discarded, heavy gin fan and throws it into the back of the pickup where it bounces off something bulky concealed under a tarpaulin. The bulk moves causing the black man to jump back.

"What that is, Boss? It be movin'!"

"Shit! Ain't nothin' but a deer I killed last night." J.W. beckons to Roy and Melvin to get into the cab of the truck. With one strong arm and hand on the fender, J.W. leaps into the back of the truck, lifts the tarpaulin and fires a shot from his .45 Colt Automatic into Emmett's head. Milam then drives the truck across the railroad track and down a street past a quaint brick church where white people, including big land owners, will soon be worshipping, totally unaware of what has happened in the bayou next to their church.

(Glendora United Methodist Church: Beside Black Bayou)

On Sunday, August 28, 1955, worshipers at this beautiful little church in Glendora, Mississippi had no idea of the horrendous crime that had played out beside their church in the waters of Black Bayou. The sermon this day could have been for J.W. Milam, if it had been based on KJV Luke 17:2: "It were better for him that a millstone were hanged about his neck, and he cast into the sea, than that he should offend one of these little ones."

Black Bayou Bridge

August 28, 1955: With a heavy gin fan tied around his neck with barbed wire, the brutalized body of Emmett Till is thrust over the rusted iron bridge railing and sinks to the bottom of the muddy waters in silence. But even in death, Emmett cannot remain still. Slowly, his body bounces along underwater, tugging the gin fan with him as he skirts the muddy bottom of the bayou.

Soon, the body travels around the curve and into the waters of the Tallahatchie River, the Delta's own Davy Jones Locker. Just like the "locker" of a deep blue sea holds the skeletons of lost sailors, the Tallahatchie's murky "locker" holds the bones of black males lynched for little or no reason. Maybe these black deaths were necessary to provide entertainment for some other Delta peckerwoods, bored with guzzling moonshine, gambling, and chasing women.

Three days pass from the time Emmett is kidnapped and a seventeen-year-old fisherman, while running his trotline in the Tallahatchie River, sees feet and knees sticking up out of the water. The boy finishes running his trot line and then tells his dad what he has seen.

Tallahatchie River, close to where Emmett's body was discovered

Tallahatchie sheriff H. C. Strider is called to the scene as well as a black undertaker from Greenwood and Emmett's Uncle Mose Wright. Mose identifies the mutilated corpse as his nephew, mostly by the silver signet ring he is wearing.

Sheriff Strider orders Emmett's body to be buried the same day in Mose Wright's church cemetery at East Money. But before the body can be buried, Mamie Till receives a call from the mother of Curtis Jones, another cousin visiting Mississippi from Chicago, and Mamie is told what is happening. Mamie calls her uncle Crosby Smith in Sumner, who contacts the sheriff of Leflore County and has the burial stopped. Mamie's son's body is shipped to Chicago for burial.

The world would never forget Emmett Till! Nor would they put out of their minds the cruel way in which he died!

Whore's Lake outside Drew, MS

Whore's Lake hides its gruesome, heart wrenching past in a picturesque, serene location a short distance down the road from the wooden seed barn outside Drew. In Ruth Jackson's book *Whore's Lake*, she retells stories passed down, about the lake being a dumping place for black women who were beaten, raped, and murdered by white men. One white man stood out from the rest in these horrendous crimes. Sheriff "Big John", the law in Drew, was described by Jackson as a serial rapist and murderer of African American women, teenage girls, and even little girls. Once he raped and killed the black females, he would "piss" on them and leave their bodies beside Whore's Lake.

Susan Orr-Klopfer goes further telling how the men of the KKK would use black women as their own personal prostitutes until their wives found out. The wives would then murder the black women and throw their bodies in Whore's Lake, an act of revenge the wives should have directed toward their unfaithful husbands.

Photographs of Black Bayou Bridge Courtesy of C. Hanchey

Black Bayou Bridge

The bridge was placed on the National Register of Historic Places in 2011.

Chapter Six

The Trial and the "Confession"

Based on information given to the sheriff of Leflore County by Mose Wright, Roy Bryant was arrested for kidnapping Emmett on the afternoon of August 28, 1955. A short time later, J.W. Milam made sure he, too, was arrested so he could be in jail with Roy. The family, under matriarch Eula Lee (Milam) Bryant, feared Roy might not stick to the story they had concocted. Carolyn Bryant and her two small sons were hidden in different family members' houses in several locations where she was drilled in what she was to say should Roy and J.W. stand trial for Emmett's murder. Carolyn was not allowed to talk to anyone, not even her birth family, something which alarmed her family members who were told by Eula Lee and her other children, Carolyn did not want to talk to them.

"Too bad you left the pistol in the car," Eula Lee told Carolyn. "You coulda saved 'em all the trouble."

Eula Lee Bryant was a hard woman who ruled her clan of five boys and three girls. The children were from two husbands: the first a Milam who died as a result of a work-related accident; the second a much younger man (only 18 when she married him) named Bryant who ran off with another woman, leaving Eula to take care of her large brood of children. Eula Lee drank whiskey for breakfast, played cards and gambled, and always packed a pistol in her purse, according to Carolyn Bryant's "confess all" to Timothy Tyson. Eula Lee Bryant hoped to run into her sorry ex-husband some day, and when she did, she swore she'd use that .38 on him.

After Emmett's body was discovered in the river, J.W. Milam and Roy Bryant remained in jail. The Grand Jury in Sumner listened to the evidence and sent J.W. Milam and Roy Bryant to trial in

September 1955, for the kidnapping and murder of Emmett Till. The trial lasted five days but the conviction of the two white men proved impossible to obtain. Every lawyer in Sumner defended the two white men, and collections were taken up all over three counties for their defense fund.

But the deciding factor in the two men's acquittal proved to be H. C. Strider, sheriff of Tallahatchie County, a big farmer with an even bigger ego and the demand to be in control. On August 31st when the body was pulled from the Tallahatchie River, Sheriff Strider agreed with the identification Mose Wright gave: the body was kidnap victim Emmett Till. But during the murder trial, Strider convinced everyone, especially the jury, the body was not Emmett Till because it had been in the water far longer than three days. He also convinced the jury the whole thing was a conspiracy concocted by the northern NAACP to undermine the southern way of life. The jury found the defendants not guilty.

Two witnesses, Henry Lee Loggins and Two Tight Collins, could have possibly swayed the jury against the defendants, but they could not be found to testify. Journalist James L. Hicks, along with Dr. H.R.M. Howard of Mound Bayou, and civil rights activist Medgar Evers had followed information given in confidence and felt the two men Loggins and Collins were being hidden under fictitious names in the jail in Charleston or in other jails in the area. Oddly, Henry Loggins' wife was the one who told Hicks Henry Lee was involved. At the time, she was pregnant with Henry Lee Loggins' child. One of his sons grew up to be Johnny B. Thomas, the mayor of Glendora and the director of the Emmett Till Historic and Intrepid Center, a museum filled with memorabilia and information about Emmett Till.

Milam and Bryant, once acquitted of Emmett's murder, knew they could not be tried for this crime a second time. In December, three months later, they confessed to Emmett's murder to movie producer and journalist William Bradford Huie who agreed to pay Bryant and Milam $4000 for their confession which appeared in *Look* Magazine in January 1956. In the article "The Shocking Story of Approved Killing in Mississippi", lies and discrepancies make up the majority of the so called confession.

Milam, who did the confessing for himself and his brother, mentioned no white accomplices and no black hired men. Milam painted Emmett as a strong-willed, surly young man who showed no remorse for disrespecting Roy's young wife. In fact, the men maintained Emmett was boastful of "having white women" right up until they shot him and threw his body in the river with a seventy-pound gin fan tied around his neck.

In the *Look* article, Milam was described as a hero in World War II who was just preserving the dignity of southern white womanhood and protecting his superior white society against mixing with the mongrel black race. Milam was especially opposed to black communist infiltrators from the North, even a communist in the guise of a fourteen-year-old boy. The article best describes J.W. Milam's thinking about African Americans in the following statement:

> Milam: "Well, what else could we do? He was hopeless. I'm no bully; I never hurt a nigger in my life. I like niggers -- in their place -- I know how to work 'em. But I just decided it was time a few people got put on notice. As long as I live and can do anything about it, niggers are gonna stay in their place. Niggers ain't gonna vote where I live. If they did, they'd control the government. They ain't gonna go to school with my kids. And when a nigger gets close to mentioning sex with a white woman, he's tired o' livin'. I'm likely to kill him. Me and my folks fought for this country, and we got some rights. I stood there in that shed and listened to that nigger throw that poison at me, and I just made up my mind. 'Chicago boy,' I said, 'I'm tired of 'em sending your kind down here to stir up trouble. Goddam you, I'm going to make an example of you -- just so everybody can know how me and my folks stand.'"

The article in *Look* backfired on the murderers, turning the people of Tallahatchie and surrounding counties against Milam and

Bryant and causing great economic and social consequences for their families. Their stores failed, local banks refused them loans, and the community members ostracized them. Some of the family attempted to live outside the state for a while. Both marriages suffered with Roy and Carolyn divorcing and J.W. and Juanita becoming estranged, even within their own home. As Roy Bryant once said on a radio show interview, "Emmett Till ruined my life." In the same interview, Roy Bryant said "Emmett Till is dead. I don't know why he can't just stay dead?"

In her book *Death of Innocence*, Mamie Till-Mobley explained how she was listening in on the interview between the radio host and Roy Bryant and could not believe Bryant's vulgarity, his obvious hatred of her son, and his lack of remorse. Mamie, opposed to capital punishment, never wanted her son's murderers executed but she did want justice and hoped the men would be remorseful for their terrible crime. She got neither wish.

Sumner Courthouse where Milam and Bryant were acquitted of murder of Emmett Till.

On September 23, 1955, J.W. Milam and Roy Bryant walked down these stairs as free men, acquitted of the murder of Emmett Till. However, a different Jury of One would decide their fate—in the hereafter! J.W. Milam and Roy Bryant never showed remorse for killing Emmett Till.

Part II

White Feathers from Emmett

Chapter Seven

White Feather #1

 While researching Emmett's murder, I became fixated on one part, but it was not the murder itself that consumed me. Emmett's torture played over and over in my mind; sleep eluded me as I tried to imagine this young boy's pain and suffering—his head battered, his skull split in two, one eye dislodged, both wrists bones fractured, his femur broken, and shot through the head just to make sure he was dead. Consider, these are only the major wounds from his torture as reported in the FBI's autopsy report in 2005. With the reopening of the case sixty years after the trial, Emmett's body was exhumed and the autopsy, never performed in 1955, was finally performed. Contrary to Sheriff Strider's defense strategy which ultimately led to the acquittal of J.W. Milam and Roy Bryant, the autopsy proved, once and for all, the body found in the Tallahatchie River was that of fourteen-year-old Emmett Till. The brutality of Emmett's torture and murder could no longer be denied. Cause of death was reported as a gunshot wound to the head.

 Reading Mamie Till Mobley's <u>Death of Innocence</u> proved difficult; it was hard to read through tear-filled eyes, with a heart overflowing with compassion. How did Mamie have the strength to not only examine her son's mutilated body from feet to head, but to allow others to see her once beautiful boy as a grotesque corpse? As Mamie said to the undertaker in Chicago when he asked if she wanted him to touch up the body, "No, let the world see what I see; I want them to see what they did to my boy."

 I went to the Delta to learn about Emmett Till and I learned much about myself.

Dr. Sue

White Feathers from Emmett

First Visit to Glendora, Mississippi

On February 26, 2017, I received a comforting answer to my preoccupation with Emmett's pain and suffering—had I recognized its meaning at the time. With the museum closed, the only building open at Glendora was the agricultural Quonset hut sitting in front of the Emmett Till Historical and Intrepid Center. The Quonset hut looks as old as the museum that served as a cotton gin from 1950 to 1956 under the ownership of M.E. Lowe *(see reference to warranty deed under Works Consulted)*. While my friends were walking around reading the Emmett Till signs, I was drawn to the giant open Quonset hut. As soon as I entered the structure, an eerie feeling crept over me—a feeling I have experienced many times in historical places such as this. My heart beat out its own Morse Code tapping, "You are not alone!"

Inside the Quonset Hut (February 26, 2017)

The wind blows through the tall open structure, the metal sides screeching— perhaps from age, perhaps from remembering a horrendous event beginning and ending here in 1955. With my research efforts into the Till murder just beginning, I find myself wishing I knew more details surrounding Emmett's murder. Although my expectations have little knowledge base, my years of experience with the paranormal tell me anything, or at least something, is possible here. An uncanny chill races back and forth, heart to head—head to heart as the vibes beat louder than my heart.

"Emmett, are you here?"

The metal sides pitch and whine, seeming ready to bend and break as the wind passes through the expanse like spirits chasing each other in play. I stall; a loud noise renders my body immobile even though the bang is silent to my ears. I feel the small, inexpensive camcorder I have aimed at nothing and everything holds secrets to be divulged later when listening back and watching footage downloaded from the SDHC card. Everything that happens this first visit will have great meaning—if I can decipher what I've recorded.

As I listen to and watch the footage that night, I hear two voices. One sounds like a young boy who gives a plea for help in a sing-song voice like song lyrics, possibly an attempt to avoid stuttering. What he asks could determine his last possibility for escape.

"Help me! You're the one brought me!"

With my heart racing, I increase the volume in iMovie to 400 percent, hoping to hear the answer to his plea for help. A deep male voice answers, the first words repeated in a slight stutter of his own.

"I can't...I can't get in trouble...wi' the boss!"

Inside the Quonset hut that afternoon, I continue to watch, listen, and video, and after a few minutes, my friend Belinda comes into the Quonset hut and is startled by something.

"What is it?" I ask the question, and she points to a bird that has flown in over us and perches in the rafters looking down as if watching—or listening.

"It's a dove!" I tell Belinda. And with that revelation, the dove leaves its perch and flies out the other end.

Frank, Belinda's husband, comes in and I ask him if he feels anything. Frank is often sensitive in places like this. He, too, has cold chills, and I ask him to move to the spot producing the most pronounced chills—hair standing up on his arms or the back of his neck. Frank finds the spot and I make sure my camera is focused on him. While watching and listening to the footage later, I hear the same deep male voice at the location where Frank has stopped but I cannot understand the words.

The next words I speak surprise me. I do not know where these words came from since I know so little about Emmett Till. Did my brain hear a bang or something, and react to what my ears did not hear? As Belinda and I listen to the footage later, a loud bang is heard.

"This is where he died, Frank. This is where he died!" I blurt out the words but have no idea from where they originated.

A voice is recorded, sounding like Emmett's but this voice is a little gravelly.

"This is it."

Could this be Emmett verifying once and for all this is where he took his last breath? The voice is so similar to the one recorded a few minutes earlier.

I stay probably twenty minutes total in the agricultural expanse and find it hard to leave. Frank waits patiently inside the hut, and Belinda stands in the doorway, looking down with her phone camera aimed at something.

"Here's your white feather!"

"Huh?" I hear Belinda but need time to process. This can't be real! As I say in the introduction, in my seventy-two years of life, I have never found a white feather in my path. Yet, white feathers are very important to me.

In two of my novels, I have used a white feather sent to earth as comfort for loved ones left grieving, a message from the one passed. In *Wings on Mountain Breezes*, hero Custer, a Native American, sends the white tail feather from the eagle, his animal spirit, to assure his grieving widow he is okay and at peace and she should be, too. The feather is important in this book as a grand finale, the last book in this five book series with The Wild Rose Press, a series I began writing twelve years ago.

Probably, my most poignant use of the white feather is in the young adult paranormal mystery *Freeze Tag* in which an eight-year-old girl Lilly finds a white feather on her mother's grave.

Excerpt from *Freeze Tag*:

We hurry to her side and look where she is pointing. A single white feather lies atop Mom's grave in front of her tombstone. Lilly picks the feather up and caresses her cheek with it.

"It's Mom's sign!" Lilly clasps her hands and shivers in excitement.

"What sign, Lilly?" As soon as I ask the question, I remember Mom's words:

I don't think dead people become angels. I think God already has angels in place when we get to heaven. But I'll let you know, or rather, Lilly will let you know. We have an agreement.

"It's from an angel wing. Mom's an angel! See, Anna!" Lilly takes the feather and holds it out to me. I take it and copy Lilly's action rubbing my cheek with the long white plume layered with hundreds of small, down feathers. As I pass the feather beneath my nose, I smell it--Mom's Palmolive soap, a sign just for me.

"I think you're right, Lilly." I smile and hand the feather back to my sister. "Mom said she'd send you a sign, didn't she? Is this the sign she promised?" Lilly nods her head signifying it is and gives a faint smile as she wipes a tear from her cheek. I hug my little sister but I do not cry. Instead, I look up to heaven and smile.

End

A white feather is a gift from a loved one delivered with God's approval and/or help. It symbolizes peace, love, and joyous living on earth and in the hereafter with our Lord and Savior. A white feather should never be overlooked or scoffed at as unimportant. Each one is better than a penny from heaven; it is a gift transported by angels. Yes, birds molt and lose feathers all the time, even white feathers, but where their feathers fall can be significant in the heavenly realm of things. My heart and soul tell me this is true.

I walk to where Belinda is standing and there right at the entrance to the hut lies a white feather, blowing in the breeze. As I pick it up, my video camera catches the same young male voice whispering.

"I'm here getting loved."

With the first white feather found at the Quonset hut, I feel Emmett is reassuring me he is at peace, in heaven, with Mamie and all those who loved him on earth, and he is telling me to stop dwelling on what happened to him. When he whispered "I'm here getting loved", I felt he was telling me he was in heaven being loved until I visited one of my favorite historical homes in Mississippi, Rowan Oak, the home of William Faulkner in Oxford.

I had sent the YouTube link of the voices recorded in the

Quonset hut to Bill, curator of Rowan Oak, an acquaintance of mine and someone who seems interested in what I catch on my video camera, especially when I catch voices at Rowan Oak. Not long ago, we were discussing the voices from my first visit to the Emmett Till sites and I told Bill what I thought Emmett was telling me.

    Bill studied my reaction and then explained his theory. "No, I don't think he is telling you he is in heaven being loved at all. Emmett is saying he is being loved by you—right here and right there in that Quonset hut."

    I fought the tears welling behind my eyes and realized Bill was telling me the truth. Even though I never knew Emmett in the physical world we shared for a while, I do love Emmett Till and will never forget him. Emmett is special to me and each time I go to one of the sites that memorialize him now, I remember Bill's prophetic words.

Watch "White Feathers from Emmett: White Feather #1" at YouTube link: https://youtu.be/1oc4M7YLhc4

Quonset hut visited on Feb. 26, 2017, by Dr. Sue and friends Belinda and Frank:

Dr. Sue believes Emmett might have taken his last breath here after being shot in the head, a final blow to Emmett's already tortured, mangled body. EVP's (Electronic Voice Phenomenon) were recorded by Dr. Sue on her video camera and were clearly understood when footage was downloaded on her computer and listened to that night by Dr. Sue and Belinda.

Quonset hut (right) is now enclosed. The Emmett Till Historical and Intrepid Center was once the old Glendora Cotton Gin from which Milam took the gin fan that was tied around Emmett's neck with barbed wire before his body was dumped in Black Bayou.

"Emmett, did you hear the train that morning you were in the back of Milam's parked truck? Did you long to be on the northbound train—on your way back to Chicago to your mama?" These were the words Dr. Sue spoke to Emmett in the Quonset hut as the train passed on the track just outside the open doorways.

Chapter Eight

White Feather #2

My second visit to the Emmett Till sites took place on April 15, 2017. With friends Hilda and Belinda, we headed for Sumner for a guided tour. With Jessie Jaynes from Mississippi Delta Experience Touring as our guide, we hoped to accomplish the following: tour the Sumner Courthouse; visit the Emmett Till Historical and Intrepid Center at Glendora; find the Black Bayou Bridge where Keith Beauchamp and others believe Emmett's body was dumped; and check out the seed barn on the old Shurden Plantation just outside Drew, the spot Keith thought had the greatest potential for activity. Emmett was taken to the seed barn around 6:30 a.m. on August 28, 1955, was tortured, and was shot in the head ending his life, or so many believe.

This is Hilda's first trip and Belinda's and my second trip to the Emmett Till sites, but I wanted the two of them to know as much as possible about the Till case. The best way to do this was to get Keith Beauchamp to tell the story. Keith was gracious enough to give us a history lesson by speaker phone, all the way from my house in Yalobusha County to Sumner in West Tallahatchie County. Not only did Keith summarize a half lifetime worth of investigating what actually happened to Emmett in the Delta in 1955, he disclosed many little known details about the case. We sat mesmerized by this young filmmaker's knowledge.

Keith set the stage for my most enlightening visit to the Till sites. His prediction about the seed barn at Drew being potentially active, proved to be true and another white feather was presented in my own quest.

Jessie guided us first through the beautiful old courthouse

at Sumner where once again, a voice was caught, this time in front of the double doors leading into the courtroom just before entering. The voice was distinct, somewhat deep, very southern, and terribly demanding.

"Get off the phone!" The man did not ask politely but gave a direct order, one he fully expected to be obeyed. No men were present in our group or anywhere in the courthouse. Even though cell phones did not exist in 1955, the man behind the voice certainly knew what the small object was—probably from the busloads of tourists who invade his domain each year. From experience, I know whatever is behind intelligent voices knows what many present day objects are such as Maglites, K-2 meters, motion detectors, and many of the novelty items used for "ghost hunting" even if they were unavailable during their lifetimes. For example, when using Maglites at Betsy Bell Powell's grave, I often record voices telling me, "Turn the light on." Maglites did not exist in the 1800's!

Of course, none of us heard the voice in the courthouse since it was an EVP, electronic voice phenomenon. But once it was recorded and we listened to it play back, we began to speculate as to who it might be.

My first thought was Sheriff H.C. Strider, the 270 pound, wealthy landowner from Tallahatchie County who was at the end of his four-year term as sheriff. (Mississippi Sheriffs could not serve more than four years after being elected). On a side note, after Strider's term ended in 1956, Harry Dogan was elected sheriff and after him in 1960, Ellett Dogan would serve as sheriff. Ironically, Ellett had married a beautiful, gracious little southern lady named Lanell Nelson who had been my aunt by marriage, widowed by my uncle T.D. Nelson's death during World War II. And after Ellett's four- year-term ended, Lanell was elected sheriff and took her job very seriously.

Sheriff Strider ruled his court with a tight fist, making sure segregation was maintained in his court. Whites were given the majority of the seats with a few black spectators sitting in back rows or standing around the walls. Each day, over two hundred spectators crowded into the courtroom for the historical media event. I would not have been surprised if we had caught Strider's daily greeting to black journalists on the video camera.

"Good mornin', niggas!" The burly man would nod as he passed by the crowded card table on the outside of the railing (white journalists were at two large tables on the other side of the railing beside the lawyers' table). Sheriff Strider set the stage for the court's proceedings convincing the jury the body found in the Tallahatchie River could not be Emmett Till. Strider insisted the corpse was planted by the NAACP, right down to placing the silver ring on the finger, a ring known to be Emmett's and identified by Mose Wright when Emmett's bloated, disfigured body lay in a boat on the bank of the Tallahatchie River. Oddly, Sheriff Strider had agreed with Mose Wright about the body being Emmett Till on the day the body was removed from the river to the bank.

The potential voice of the guardian of the courtroom, whoever he might be, would not be the only paranormal activity recorded. While in the jury deliberation room located behind the jury box, a strange shadow was videoed sitting at the head of the table. Perhaps, it was the foreman eyeing the intruders with their beloved handheld gadgets, including cell phones used as cameras. *(To compare Sheriff Strider's voice with the EVP, watch the YouTube "30th Anniversary of Emmett Till's Death" cited in Works Consulted in Appendix of this book).*

Another voice, a female, said, "Pepsi", something I cannot explain unless it was the soda supplied to the jury. Refreshments and smokes were what the jurymen used to delay giving their verdict, just to make it look like it took them longer to deliberate, a "suggestion" to the foreman attributed to Sheriff Elect Harry Dogan. The jury had their verdict in a little over an hour.

Next stop was Glendora where the museum was open. The exhibits were interesting but I was anxious to get inside the Quonset hut again to see if I could catch Emmett's voice as I had the first visit. A strange banging sound followed by what sounded like a cry of severe pain were recorded, but Hilda and I only stayed a few minutes in the hut. Children could be heard playing across the tracks, possible noise pollution for videoing.

Regardless, I was anxious to find Black Bayou Bridge on the outskirts of town. This is where Keith Beauchamp (phone interview) and Mayor Johnny B. Thomas both believe Emmett's body was dumped with a seventy-pound gin fan tied around his neck with barbed wire. The body then floated down the bayou, around a curve, and downstream into the Tallahatchie River where it was spotted by a fisherman three days later. (Watch Mayor Thomas in YouTube "My Father Helped Kill Emmett Till: Healing from the Sins of Thy Father", Part 1 of 2).

As we approached the old rusted bridge, we were in awe of the peace and serenity surrounding the setting. Virginia creeper clung to the bushes beside the old rusted trellises of the bridge and twisted its way around everything in its path, much like Emmett has wound his way around and into my mind and heart. And just like this vine, this brutally murdered young boy refuses to loose his hold on me—not yet anyway. No voices were recorded here but the emotion I felt told me I would come back.

The last stop on this trip was the long, wooden seed barn on the old Shurden Plantation a short distance outside Drew. The property is now owned by Dr. Jeff and Penny Andrews, a place Penny told us they "had their eye on for along time" before buying it in 1994. The setting proved to be one of the most beautiful spots I've seen in the Delta. It is hard to imagine the brutal crime committed here in 1955, when gazing at the pristine bayou full of ancient cypress knees forming the perfect Delta backdrop for this magnificent home sitting in the middle of an immaculate, well groomed landscape.

The shed was open and Jessie assured us the owners allow people to look in the shed. However, Jessie might not have known I would crawl around inside the back of the shed carrying on a conversation with Emmett Till. I was delighted when Jessie, too, began conversing with Emmett.

With my video camera recording, I began with my usual, "Emmett, are you here?" Many voices were recorded, but the recording that intrigued me the most was when I heard, knock …

"Emmett" … knock … knock! Later, when I read about Emmett's passion for knock, knock jokes in *Death of Innocence*, I felt sure this was Emmett. Many times, I have recorded three knocks when asking Emmett to knock, but the greatest treasure was what I found just as we were about to leave the barn at the end of our tour.

"Just let me go in here again," I told Jessie as I headed back inside the side shed in the front entrance. My eyes caught something on the ground, and there it was, a white feather, the second one found at an Emmett Till site. I could not contain my excitement and called to the others showing them before going in the shed to thank Emmett.

"I found your white feather, Emmett." My excitement was met with a chuckle, the same chuckle I have recorded at four different Emmett Till sites including the Sumner courthouse where, to my knowledge, Emmett never entered.

Watch YouTube link https://youtu.be/27F3mZ2XldY for White Feather #2.

Seed Barn outside Drew, where Emmett was tortured and possibly took his last breath

Dr. Jeff and Penny Andrews store their Christmas angel in the Seed Barn where Emmett left a white feather! How appropriate!

The bayou forms a serene backdrop for the gruesome torture scene; cypress knees stand as they have stood for decades, guardians of the pristine landscape—but not of Emmett Till.

Back of seed barn where most paranormal activity and voices were recorded

Chapter Nine

Voices of Children and White Feather #3

On our third trip to the Delta, Hilda and I decided to go to the seed barn at Drew since there seems to be so much activity there, and to visit at the time when the torture took place. With permission secured from Dr. and Mrs. Andrews, and with a little trepidation, we arrived at the shed on Sunday morning, May 28, 2017, at around 6:15 a.m. We had not anticipated a thunderstorm but decided it would add to the ambience. After taking our ballpark chairs and video equipment to the back of the shed, we set up, ready for action. We would not be disappointed.

Sitting in the dark with mosquitoes buzzing around our ears, we listened to the hard raindrops. The raindrops were loud but they did not totally cover up the voices we caught. A little girl spirit was extremely playful in the opposite end from where I have caught what I believe to be Emmett's voice. The little girl's actions were intelligent which means she took part in our conversations, reacting to whatever we were talking about. Keep in mind, these were EVP's and not heard by our ears.

At one point, the little girl even joked with Hilda. Looking around in the clutter, Hilda tried to reassure herself "No self-respecting snake would be in here." The little girl jokingly replied, "Right beside that window…nothing!" Once she sang, "The rain can't go…I can go!" Another time when Hilda and I were discussing a dove we could hear, she joined in with, "Birdie sing." After we watched a nearly white dove fly away, the little girl asked, "Bird ha' left?" Black dialect was prominent in this question.

Earlier, the little girl sounded distressed with, "Mommy! Help!" This would be residual, a playback of something that happened here in another age. This is also what prompted me to add

White Feathers from Emmett

the part in the murder scene written by Jeff Gentry, where one of the participants in Emmett's murder tells of Klan wives murdering black women who are being used by Klansmen, and also of murdering little girls, possibly children born of white Klan daddies. Local lore has the black women and little girls' bodies thrown in Whore's Lake which is a short distance down the road from the barn outside Drew. Susan Orr-Klopfer and Ruth Jackson both included the tales of Whore's Lake in their books and writings.

Emmett was less talkative than the little girl but the K-2 meter went to red several times in reaction to our questions directed at him. I felt Emmett's greatest reaction to our attempt to reach him in those early morning hours was sending the almost white dove who perched on the ground right outside the large doorway at daylight. A dove, especially a white dove, symbolizes peace, and if there was a message to be gleaned from visit four, this was it. The little girl's clear voice was a bonus. I can only imagine what fun these two comical spirit children must have in the back of this old seed barn.

Although no white feather was found during the third visit, the dove played a dominant roll and became a sign of Emmett's presence on future visits to the Emmett Till sites. This trip proved to be the most rewarding for voices.

Watch the YouTube "Messages from Bobo", and then read further for White Feather #3, still part of this chapter.

Watch YouTube link: https://youtu.be/3tOLBpUc2HI for "Messages from Bobo", the session with the most voices recorded, including the little girl spirit.

Hilda takes advantage of early morning daylight to google "Game Birds of Mississippi" in search of a picture of an almost white dove who sings for us outside the seed barn.

Dr. Sue videos the beautiful flat Delta fields behind the seed barn.

Visit Number 4: White Feather #3

On the fourth visit to the Delta, my friend Belinda was with me. Since she was with me when the other two white feathers were found, the potential for finding another white feather was great.

We arrived at Emmett Till Historic and Intrepid Center at Glendora, and even though we had been through the center with tour guide Jessie, we decided to go through it again. A group of four pulled in beside us and we began talking to them.

Lee Brunetti is a high school history teacher from Kansas and with him was a group of three college age young people. Lee's daughter Kinsella was part of the group and seemed excited with all the Emmett Till information, especially since she is a senior in college majoring in history. Lee's nephews Collin and Paul also showed interest in the museum, something making me very happy being a former high school history teacher.

We stopped to view the film first before going into the museum. As Lee and I walked through looking at the exhibits, we did what history teachers do when they get together—we competed to see who knew the most about the topic of the day, Emmett Till. While we were swapping info, I told the group about the two white feathers I had been given and showed them the YouTube from the Quonset hut. They were impressed with how clear the voices of Emmett and Henry Lee Loggins were, or who I think the voices were. They had no idea what lay ahead for them.

I told them about the seed barn at Drew, and Lee was disappointed because they did not have time to go to Drew since they were heading back to Kansas. I also told him about Black Bayou Bridge and offered to lead them to it. Of course, they accepted my offer.

As we walked out on the bridge, Lee and I began talking about the brutal torture of Emmett Till and about the final shot to the head, the cause of death according to the FBI autopsy report in 2005.

As we stood talking, one of the young men in the group asked, "Is that a white feather floating down the stream?" We all moved to his end of the bridge and searched the muddy water for the feather. There, floating gently down the stream was a huge white feather!

"Oh, naw!" I said in disbelief, but this was not a small feather like the other two. This was a huge, extremely white feather, possibly from an egret or crane. I had trouble trying to focus my camera on it with the sun's glare, but did manage to capture it, although what I wanted to do was go tearing through the thick, snake-infested brush on the bank, charge into the muddy water filled not only with water moccasins but with ancient gar with teeth like alligators, and retrieve the third white feather for my feather treasure trove. I restrained myself!

Just as with feather number 2, I recorded the chuckle that could only belong to a fourteen-year-old boy who loves a good joke, or who experiences great joy when others find surprises he leaves! Even though the chuckle was quite distinct and easily recognizable by me, I wanted to make sure it was not either of the two young men on the bridge. I had to get in touch with the Kansas teacher whose name I failed to get that day so a bit of detective work was necessary.

Going back to the museum, I checked the register for June 2nd and there he was—Lee Brunetti from a town in Kansas. Immediately, I got on the internet, looked up the local high school and found his name and his email listed under faculty. BINGO!

I emailed Lee and sent him the YouTube link from the bridge and asked him to please listen carefully to the chuckle and see if it might have been one of his group. Lee had all three from his group to listen and they all agreed it was not any of them.

With THREE WHITE FEATHERS AT THREE EMMETT TILL SITES AND ANOTHER CHUCKLE IDENTICAL TO THE OTHERS RECORDED ON MY VIDEO CAMERA, the prospect of the white feathers being coincidence became exponentially LESS LIKELY! But this quest for answers was not over—yet!

Watch "White Feather #3 at YouTube link: https://youtu.be/2GfwIHj8J54 .

White Feathers from Emmett

White Feather #3 proves unreachable as it floats down snake-infested Black Bayou at Glendora, Mississippi.

Chapter Ten

A Psychic Visits the Delta

Livie is a psychic from another state and just happens to share a friend with me. When I found out our mutual friend wanted to bring Livie to Mississippi, I could not have been more pleased. As always, the opportunity availed itself at the perfect time and I was not about to pass it up.

In order to understand Livie's gift of communicating with those passed, she relies on her faith in God as the provider. As she put it on more than one occasion while visiting Mississippi, "I wear my cross as my armor to remind anything negative I might run across, that I am protected by a Higher Presence and I do not fear." However, she did say she certainly does not seek the negative forces and tries to avoid them.

I am not new to the world of psychics after writing *Through the Eyes of Angel Leigh*, but I always reserve acceptance and belief in each one through proof and personal messages delivered to me. Shortly after Livie entered my house, she gave me messages. One was from my son, and the other from my sister Minnie, both deceased. Minnie's name was in Livie's notes brought from home. Livie knew nothing about me or my family and both messages gave me great comfort.

When I found out Livie was coming, I asked our mutual friend if Livie might be interested in visiting the sites of Emmett Till since so many questions remain about the case. Through our friend, Livie sent me a message saying she would help but only if certain conditions were met:

"I want no recognition, no publicity, no monetary compensation, no pictures taken of me, no use of any information that might identify me, and most of all, I want no information beforehand, especially not names. I want to be open to receive information and do not want to risk developing preconceived notions."

I was blown away! Livie has helped the police solve cases in her state but this is not how she earns a living. Almost immediately and even at a great distance from Mississippi, Livie began receiving messages. Our friend in common delivered these messages to me.

I could not believe how much Livie knew about the Emmett Till case, and she was never given any information—not even his name. But I would have to wait a few weeks before her visit. In the meantime, I continued visiting the Emmett Till sites with my video camera in hand.

If I was going to take Livie to the Emmett sites in the order in which they happened, our first stop would be to the train station at Winona where Mose Wright, Wheeler Parker, and Emmett were met by Mose's sixteen-year-old son Maurice on August 21, 1955. Knowing Livie's time in Mississippi is limited, I decided to go in the order in which the three white feathers had been placed in my path the last four months, adding two more important sites. I believed these locations to be important in the timeline for Emmett's last hours on earth and important to what he is trying to tell me.

The remainder of this chapter is based on Livie's "seeing" at these five sites: 1) Glendora, site of Emmett Till Historical and Intrepid Center, the Quonset hut where I received the first white feather and recorded voices on my first visit, and area where Milam's house once sat; 2) Money, site of Bryant's Store and site of the Wolf Whistle; 3) the Tallahatchie River where Emmett's body was found near Philipp; 4) Black Bayou Bridge on outskirts of Glendora; 5) the wooden seed barn at Drew.

SITE 1: Glendora, Mississippi

As we approached the first stop, Livie put on a blindfold, not wanting to influence messages she might receive and to establish credibility. She never read any of the many signs posted at these sites. Once we got to the site of the Emmett Till Historical Intrepid Center, the Quonset hut, and site of J.W. Milam's house, Livie took the blindfold off and began walking around, spending most of her time at the site of Milam's house. The Quonset Hut was off limits since it was enclosed.

Following are notes taken from the video footage at Glendora and other sites. Keep in mind Livie had no foreknowledge except it is a criminal case. She had already said it happened a long time ago. Unless otherwise noted, statements are direct quotes made by Livie but without quotation marks. After Livie's quotes, I placed information and possible explanations in italics. Some of Livie's messages remain unexplained but I have faith they will be.

Livie's Messages
Site 1: Glendora

1) There are many stories to tell—many are scared to talk. (*Dr. Sue: This is still true of Glendora and Money; most people here, especially African Americans, do not like to talk to strangers about the Emmett Till case*).
2) (*Before we cross the track at Glendora*) Something happened at a railroad track—by a railroad track.

    Dr. Sue: The major Emmett Till sites at Glendora are all right beside the railroad track with the exception of the bridge. Also, this is the site where a couple of months after the Milam/Bryant trial, Elmer Kimbrell, or Kimbell, who was possibly involved in the Emmett Till murder, shot and killed a black man named Clinton Melton at a service station by the railroad. The dispute was over the amount of gas pumped into Kimbrell's car. Kimbrell refused to pay for the gas and told Melton he was leaving to get a gun and would come back and shoot him. A few minutes later, Kimbrell came back and shot and killed Clinton Melton.

    Kimbrell was arrested but was out on bond immediately, stood trial, and was found not guilty by reason of self defense even though the service station owner witnessed the shooting. Kimbrell had gone to J.W. Milam's house after shooting Melton and somehow ended up with a bullet wound in his shoulder, something suspect since Clinton Melton was unarmed.

Beulah Melton, wife of the victim, was killed in a wreck four days before Kimbrell's trial. Her car ran off the road into Black Bayou where she drowned. Her two youngest children (of four total) were with her and were rescued. The citizens of the community let it be known they condemned Kimbrell's murder of Melton and gave assistance to Beulah before her death. Many believe she was run off the road but it was never proven.

3) (*Blindfold off*) Where's the store? They (*voices*) are saying, "Take me to the store." (*Dr. Sue: This is probably a reference to Bryant's Store where we are going next*).
4) There are people out playing checkers. (*Again, this is probably Bryant's Store in Money*).
5) An African American woman is coming through and has on an apron—says she is breaking beans.
6) Stove, avocado green with a round clock in center
7) Person drowned; dunked him in the water (*Dr. Sue: This is probably a reference to Emmett but could be others who were lynched*).
8) Tiberius—having pain
9) Little sister? Woman with little girl crying…heavyset woman (*Dr. Sue: This could be Beulah Melton but this is not known for sure since I have not found a picture of Mrs. Melton*).
10) Shining flashlights (*Dr. Sue: This is most likely a reference to Emmett Till's torture and murder since he was brought to Glendora, according to Milam's telephone interview with Bonnie Blue. Milam and the others used flashlights throughout the abduction, torture, and murder because the night was especially dark*).
11) Getting the tar beat out of him (*Dr. Sue: This is most likely referring to Emmett*).
12) Car with big hood similar to one below: (*Dr. Sue: I do not know who this could belong to but would love to know what kind of car Hubert Clark had in 1955*).

13) Does a person involved have a farm—and a long barn on it? *(Dr. Sue: This has to be a reference to the seed barn at Drew where we are going later).*

14) They *(negative voices at site where Milam's house stood)* are threatening me: "You won't get away with this, little bitch…butting in where you don't belong…trespassing…leave well enough alone!" This man was a bully when he was alive. *(Dr. Sue: This has to be J.W. Milam).*

SITE 2: Ruins of Bryant's Store at Money, Mississippi

1) This is where they played checkers. *(Holds her arm out)* Look—the hair is standing up on my arm. *(Dr. Sue: Young people were playing checkers in front of Bryant's Store the night of the Wolf Whistle incident, and Emmett's group of young people joined them).*

2) Did this have a wood stove in it? *(Dr. Sue: A local man said he knew there was a fireplace in the apartment behind the store but did not know about a stove).*

3) I'm getting initial B—was someone involved with initial B? *(Dr. Sue: B was for Bryant).*

4) They *(negative voices)* are calling me a charlatan *(a fake or quack, something Livie is NOT).*

5) Where's the door where you had to knock a certain way to get in? *(Dr. Sue: This could be a possible KKK connection or, possibly, used when selling moonshine, something Milam was known to do).*
6) Somebody being manhandled...

    Dr. Sue: Two possibilities exist. Roy manhandled a young boy who came into the store, thinking it was the Chicago boy until the boy's mother questioned Roy's action and Carolyn said it was not him. Carolyn was manhandled by Roy when he found out she had not told him about the whistling incident, something he said shamed him not knowing when others knew all about it).
7) More threats... "Have you lost your mind? Dredging up things better left alone...we don't like people like you... all fun and games until someone gets hurt."
8) I hear "peaches" and "Larry" but don't know what this means.
9) Good voices are telling me, "Put on your armor!" They know my cross is my armor.
10) Do these people still have family alive?

    Dr. Sue: Milam and Bryant's descendants still live in the area in Tallahatchie, Leflore, Sunflower, and Panola Counties plus other counties in the state; all I know of are fine people, many well educated with established and honorable professions, and they are good citizens who like all of us, including myself, are still "paying for the sins of our fathers", or kinfolks from another era.
11) More went on in that store than just people playing checkers!

    Dr. Sue: J.W. Milam had been in trouble for selling moonshine; Roy got in trouble later for food stamp fraud but not at this store; criminal plotting of any kind was possible with these ruthless men. The FBI tried to prove a KKK connection but it was never proven. However, in Susan Orr-Klopfer's THE EMMETT TILL BOOK, Susan told of a girl, kin to one of the brothers by marriage, who knew both Milam and Bryant well, and said the two were members of the KKK. Susan conducted interviews all over the Delta when she and her husband lived at Parchman, and she gathered information no one else had been able to uncover).

12) Was a men thing—making plans in the store—a lot of talk but only to certain people. *(See remarks above).*
13) I am shown men's feet—four pair of shoes. *(Dr. Sue: Later, Livie sent me a picture of shoes like ones she saw... see picture following):*

SITE 3: Tallahatchie River where Emmett's body was found near Philipp, Mississippi

Once again, Livie puts on her blindfold and keeps it on until we stop to get out at the bridge. On the way, and several times during this stop and the rest of the day, Livie hears voices singing, "We shall be free." This could be a reference to civil rights songs or songs sung by slaves. In a modern sense, Garth Brooks wrote a song in recent years with this title. In it, he is against racism and violence and thinks we should all embrace our differences as a people and live in harmony. Garth said he received criticism for the song but wanted the world to know not everyone is a racist, even if they like, or sing, country music.

1) A man is saying, "And the truth shall set you free." *(Dr. Sue: This could be reference to songs sung for Civil Rights or to Bible verses; Livie explained these were African American spirits who were showing her support).*
2) I see a house, brick with iron railing.
3) *(Livie, speaking aloud to a negative voice who does not want her here)* I'm not afraid of you.

4) I see shoes again but I'm not allowed to see faces.

   Dr. Sue: At one point, Livie mentioned seeing white, suggesting possible KKK activity, but the Klan did not always wear white robes, wanting to be more discreet, and Livie actually says this later; the White Citizens Council, created in Indianola, Mississippi in 1954 and made up mostly of professionals, did not dress in white robes but they did hire the Klan to do dirty work on occasion since the Citizens Council members did not want to soil their hands...or their "good names")!

5) A man is trying to come through who was hung on a tree. *(Dr. Sue: Could be any number of lynching victims since there were hundreds in the past century).*

6) Man in overalls, smoking, sitting under a tree—African American man with short beard and mustache, a guy who worked the land; they are calling me "Miss Livie" and he says, "They said you were coming." *(Dr. Sue: Livie explained how many times, the spirits know she is coming).*

7) My stomach is killing me!

8) They are saying, "There's lots of us here!"

   Dr. Sue: Hundreds of lynchings of black people occurred in Mississippi in past centuries, some open to public viewing; a common saying for people like Milam was, "There's plenty of room in the Tallahatchie for more niggas!" We will never know how many black people were disposed of in this and other rivers and lakes in the state).

9) I see a boat with somebody sitting on the side of it.

   Dr. Sue: On the morning of August 31, 1955, three days after Emmett's abduction, a pair of knees and feet bobbing in the water were spotted by young fisherman Robert Hodges while checking his trotlines on the Tallahatchie. The sheriff was called by Hodge's father and two boats were used to bring Emmett's body to the bank since his body was weighed down with a gin fan full of mud from the bottom of the river).

10) There's danger! Someone tied to something and slipped ... *(Dr. Sue: This could be a reference to Emmett with the gin fan*

tied around his neck, or to the body tied to a rope and dragged by the feet as his body is towed to the bank. Emmett's body was caught on a snag when it was discovered).

11) Victim had on white shirt. *(Dr. Sue: Emmett was dressed in a white shirt, gray pants, and his penny loafers when he was abducted).*

12) African Americans say, "Whatever happened here has moved mountains!" Again they sing, "We shall be free." *(Dr. Sue: Yes, indeed and I repeat Mamie's words: "Emmett was the catalyst for the Civil Rights Movement.)"*

Bridge on Tallahatchie River close to where Emmett's body was brought to the bank…maybe!

13) Something was passed around.

Dr. Sue: This could mean several things but most likely is Emmett's silver signet ring with initials L.T. engraved on it. It was Emmett's deceased father's ring Emmett wore for the first time on his trip to Mississippi. Mose Wright identified Emmett's body by the ring. The ring disappeared during or after the trial and has never been found.

Finding Emmett's ring could be my mission, what Emmett is guiding me to do. If I should find it, it would have to go to Emmett's family, the rightful owners, but I would hope it would be donated to the Civil Rights Exhibit in the Smithsonian where his original casket is on exhibit. For some reason, I think the time is right for the ring to be returned.

Emmett's silver signet ring *(Drawing based on pictures found)*

SITE 4: Seed barn on old Shurden Plantation where Emmett was tortured and possibly murdered outside Drew, Mississippi
1) Tall guy with sandy hair—slightly thinning or receding.
2) Who is Price?

> *Dr. Sue: The only possible explanation I could give Livie was Cecil Price, deputy who was convicted of participating in kidnapping and murder of Schwerner, Chaney, and Goodman in the 1964 civil rights slayings in Philadelphia, Mississippi. Once again, this could be a reference to KKK involvement since Cecil Price was in the KKK. Another possibility is one man on the jury in Milam and Bryant's trial had the last name Price, a man from Charleston, but I have found no additional*

information on this person in connection with the Emmett Till case.
3) *The (African Americans) keep singing, "We shall be free."*
4) *Someone with a strong hand—controlling*

    Dr. Sue: Obviously, this is Milam but could be Roy Bryant although he had a quieter, deceiving manner about him. It could also be Sheriff Strider who wanted to control everything in Tallahatchie County. He ran the courtroom for Milam and Bryant's trial with an iron fist and insulted black journalists and U.S. Senator Diggs.

5) People had been drinking—a lot of courage comes with liquor. *(Dr. Sue: All the white men had been drinking and playing cards; they particularly liked to drink moonshine. According to Carolyn Bryant Donham in Tyson's book, the Bryant/Milam men, and their mother were all big drinkers).*
6) I feel something happened in both corners of the barn *(Dr. Sue: Back parts of the seed barn in both corners are where many voices and activity were recorded).*
7) There was a beating. *(Dr. Sue: This probably refers to the brutal torture of Emmett but could be other black people as well, or even Roy's abusive treatment of his wife Carolyn).*
8) Something is missing; there should be something like someone could be tied to but it's not here anymore—something on walls, too.

    Dr. Sue: The present owner Dr. Andrews said the FBI thoroughly investigated the barn in 2005 and found nothing like the pole described in the murder chapter. Dr. Andrews said there was no pole like this in the barn when he bought the place in 1994. If there originally, these would most likely have been taken down by Leslie Milam, not wanting any evidence Emmett was tortured in the shed. Livie's seeing this in the seed barn is what prompted my co-author Jeff Gentry and me to include it in the murder scene. With his conscience bothering him, or perhaps knowing his death was close and fearing eternal punishment, Leslie Milam made a deathbed confession to his pastor admitting to his part in Emmett's murder.

9) I heard a racist remark I don't want to say. "It's just a n-----." *(Dr. Sue: Proper terms were not in any of these men's vocabulary when it came to black people).*
10) In a text message, Livie told me: "Please see if there is a Lincoln County connection."

  On August 13, 1955, two weeks before Emmett was murdered, Lamar Smith, a sixty-three-year-old man who fought in World War I, was gunned down on the courthouse yard at Brookhaven, MS, in LINCOLN COUNTY. Smith had led a black voter registration drive which included securing absentee ballot votes for a candidate running against the incumbent supervisor in a run-off election. It was Smith's obligation to return six absentee ballots to the courthouse that day but he was intercepted by three angry white men, supporters of the incumbent supervisor. An altercation ensued and Smith was shot. According to one person interviewed in the documentary "Murder in Black and White", Smith crawled to a "green bush with red berries" where he died from the gunshot wounds.

  Even though at least thirty witnesses were present, none would give evidence against the three white men arrested. A second grand jury was convened with the same results. The men arrested for shooting Smith were Noah Smith, Mack Smith, and Charles Falvey but none stood trial.

  In the "Notice to Close File, Civil Rights Division, Department of Justice", dated April 12, 2010, information from the FBI Case Review in 2008, was included and showed the three men arrested had bribed a person close to the Lamar Smith to make sure he showed up at the courthouse on the day he was shot. This showed the subjects "had conspired to ambush the victim." By 2010, all three subjects arrested were deceased.

  No one was brought to trial for Lamar Smith's murder. The case was officially closed on April 12, 2012.

Livie received many other messages during her visit to Mississippi. Not all messages were understood at the time but are being included just in case some reader with knowledge of the case can help us determine the meanings. Other messages include the following: Richland; marching up; cook; Marshall or marshal—has to do with the crime; hollyhock (could have been "holly", a reference to the bush with red berries to which Lamar Smith crawled after being shot); names including Lance Carter, Malcom, Rufus, Hamilton, Pappy, Lucas, and Lawrence.

Hamilton could be a reference to Hermann Hamilton, an owner of a bowling alley in Denver, Colorado who was a boy nine years old in Money, Mississippi when Emmett Till was murdered. Hamilton was responsible for getting a bronze sculpture cast of Dr. Martin Luther King walking hand in hand with young Emmett Till. In Mamie Till-Mobley's book, she expressed great gratitude for the statue and was very emotional at its unveiling in Denver, Colorado in 1976. The sculpture has been moved a couple of times and is now in storage in Pueblo, Colorado.

One important message from Livie I hope to some day understand: "An older African American man knows everything."

Note: No YouTube links are listed showing Livie at the sites because of Livie's wish for anonymity. One place where she found something very important IS included in a YouTube link found in the next chapter but Livie cannot be seen in the video.

As we left the seed barn at Drew, it suddenly hit me that we had not gone to an important site while in Glendora. Coincidence? Remember! In my world, there are no coincidences! I think we were meant to go to the bridge at Black Bayou as our last stop. It would be the last Emmett Till site Livie would visit and would prove to be my signal to begin writing this book.

Chapter Eleven

Final Feather Falls

"I forgot the most important site. We have to go back to Glendora!" I announced this to the group made up of Livie and me, along with two old friends Lee and Gayle who have been on numerous paranormal investigations with me. An hour later, we returned to Glendora and made our way down the road on the opposite side of the railroad track from where we were when we made our first stop.

As we neared the path to the old bridge, we passed a beautiful old brick church, a church attended by white people, one of which is a highly respected, gracious little lady in the Glendora community. I met this lady who was with another old friend of mine, in the Sumner Grill on my first visit February 26, 2017. The lady told me how she once refused to let J.W. Milam cast his wife's vote, something he told her he had been doing for years. In fact, J.W. Milam even voted for his sister-in-law Carolyn Bryant when she turned twenty-one, something that angered Carolyn greatly since she had been looking forward to voting her first time. The lady I met from Glendora worked the polls there in the 1950's and said she did not know who J.W. Milam was at the time but it would not have made any difference. When she told the other poll watchers about the incident, they looked to see whose name had been signed and told her, "Do you know who that was? That was J.W. Milam!"

The little lady was determined to make sure everybody obeyed the rules on her poll watch. She stood her ground to one of the meanest, most domineering men to ever live in Tallahatchie County.

Dripping with sweat from the hot, humid July day, we begrudgingly left the AC in the car and trudged through the high weeds leading on to Black Bayou Bridge which played such a terrible part in the murder of Emmett Till. Ironically, or perhaps purposely, the bridge was closed shortly after Emmett's murder. It is, however, on the National Register of Historic Places, receiving this honor in 2011 as one of the last bridges of Pony Truss construction.

My mind did not seek a white feather at the bridge knowing only Emmett can decide when it is time. The time must be right—according to Emmett!

I stood on the old rusted iron bridge and gazed again into the muddy waters, receded even more now with the hot, rainless summer days, and I saw it! A beautiful white egret stood at the edge of the water. As I pointed it out to Livie and the others, the bird took flight downstream, disappearing around the curve where the bayou waters flow into the Tallahatchie River where Emmett's body floated before its discovery.

As I began telling Livie the story of my white feather journey I have followed for the past four months, she stopped me.

"Here's a white feather right here." Livie pointed to the feather at our feet and I stooped to pick it up. The central stem of the feather glistened pure white in the bright sun, and I noticed it was surrounded by sparkling silver down feathers waving around the white plume as if trying to get my attention.

"A white feather with a silver lining!" I gazed at the symbolic feather as tears filled my eyes, possibly primed by the cold chills that had replaced my overheated body only moments before.

Silence took over as on cue, the magnificent bird returned, flying gracefully back toward us, and I felt something magical happening! The bird sailed in and out of trees before zooming upward, disappearing into the top branches closest to us. I gasped and openly wept as the bird reappeared from the treetop, fluttering its much smaller white wings in rapid succession as if hurrying to meet a deadline in the white cumulus clouds above—its final destination before disappearing.

The egret had become a white dove! I looked skyward and tearfully proclaimed, "It's over! Emmett has delivered the final feather! It is time to write!"

As I wrote this chapter about the final white feather, I remembered reading a passage Mamie wrote in *Death of Innocence*, something that happened to her at Emmett's funeral in Chicago. Flipping through the book, I found the passage and again I read through moist eyes:

> There came a point in the middle of everything, as I was listening to the speakers, when I had a sensation. It was something I could just barely make out. Something fluttering somewhere. It seemed like it was in the corner of my eye, at the edge of my awareness. As my eye darted to get a better look and as my head turned to follow, the image seemed to move, just ahead of my glance, always just a flutter ahead like that, always on the borderline between conscious and subconscious. It would happen like that over and over again. And it looked to me like a dove. I wanted to see it fully, but never could. It would always move away just when I'd turn my full attention to it. I came to realize that it was a sign. The dove. A sign of peace. A sign from God.

Watch YouTube video: https://youtu.be/xmMqh-gKRFg for "Emmett's Final Feather."

Emmett's Final White Feather—this one with a silver lining!

Chapter Twelve

Summary of Scenarios

The full details of what happened that fateful morning August 28, 1955, remain sketchy. Much has been written and much more will be written attempting to answer the unanswered questions about those early morning events, but the ultimate truth is no one will ever know unless those who were present in 1955 speak from the grave! All who participated in the abduction, torture, and/or murder, or who witnessed it, are deceased except for Carolyn Bryant Donham who may or may not have been present at the abduction.

What we do know is Emmett Till was lynched. His murder was a racist hate crime—an unconscionable crime against a child whose greatest downfall was being an African American in a state and society not his home. According to documentary producer Keith Beauchamp who spent over half his life investigating the Till case, ten to fourteen people were involved in the abduction, torture, and murder.

For the purpose of this book, I have summarized scenarios using many resources *("Works Consulted" in Appendix)* in an attempt to establish a possible sequence of events, to name potential accomplices, to clarify conflicting information, and to validate many elements of the narrative including the fictionalized "Murder" from Part I. "Other" information, gained through the use of paranormal techniques including recorded voices and activity, and including information reported by psychic Livie, have been included for each major site.

Scenario One:
Preliminaries for Abduction of Emmett Till

On the night of August 27, 1955, J.W. Milam, Roy Bryant, Melvin Campbell, and most likely Hubert Clark, were drinking and playing cards in Glendora where J.W. lived. Where they were drinking remains a mystery since J.W. had owned a store in Glendora but it burned in 1954. Melvin Campbell (J.W. and Roy's brother-in-law) might have owned a store in the town but this is not known for sure. While playing cards, someone brought up the "Wolf Whistle" by the Chicago boy, and the conversation turned serious and deadly. Roy was out of state driving a truck for brother J.W. when the wolf whistle occurred, something which made Roy's reaction more volatile.

Roy found out about the incident but not from Carolyn. When he confronted her, she told him about the whistle. She had kept it from him because she knew he would get angry and might hurt the boy—or her.

It is unknown who told Roy but the most likely candidate according to Bonnie Blue's book *Emmett Till's Secret Witness*, was a huge black man named Johnny B. Washington who sometimes worked for the Bryants. Johnny B. thought he might get some extra credit or favoritism from Roy Bryant by disclosing this information. Roy became furious with Carolyn for not telling him and knocked her around for bringing shame to his house.

In the taped interview in 1985, Roy told his friend they were drinking the night of Emmett's murder, but none were drunk. Carolyn informed Timothy Tyson in his "tell all" book, Roy and the men always drank, cursed, and argued too much. After midnight the men decided it was time to avenge Roy's wife and show the Chicago boy just how things are in Mississippi. After all, J.W. and Roy were both military men, especially J.W. who had the wounds and medals from World War II to prove he was a hero and a tough man. Roy had joined the military and was a paratrooper during the Korean War but never fought in a battle or left the U.S., but he was determined to prove he was man enough to protect his woman—the same woman he often knocked around with little or no provocation.

Two Tight Collins and Henry Lee Loggins, both of whom worked for J.W. Milam, watched the card game and their white bosses as they became more vindictive with each swallow of moonshine. They both obeyed any order J.W. gave them, and Henry Lee Loggins was said to be "Milam's right hand man."

Scenario 2:
Vehicle and Accomplices in Abduction of Emmett Till

Thinking his new Chevy pickup with the white top would be too noticeable in the dark, J.W. borrowed Hubert Clark's car and off to Money some of the group headed. This is also more proof the group of kidnappers were not in J.W.'s pickup since even in the dark, the white top of the truck would have, most likely, been noticeable. Mose Wright could not tell if it was a car or pickup and did not see the white top in the dark.

J.W. and Roy were on a mission and were accompanied by Hubert Clark and/or Melvin Campbell. Also along were Two Tight Collins and Henry Lee Loggins who had been ordered to go along by Milam. Elmer Kimbrell (also known as Kimbell) was also mentioned as being involved in the violent incident since he had connections with the cotton gin at Glendora where the gin fan was taken.

From Glendora, the group headed to Preacher Mose Wright's house at East Money to kidnap Emmett. *(Refer back to preceding chapter "The Abduction.")*

Scenario 3:
Carolyn Bryant, Accomplice?

Once Milam and Bryant left Mose's house with Emmett on the morning of his torture and murder, they stopped by Bryant's Store in Money, either to take Carolyn back from Mose Wright's house after identifying Emmett as the one who insulted her three days earlier, or to take Emmett by for her to identify at the store (Carolyn's story) where she told she remained all night with her two young, sleeping sons. Mose Wright testified he heard Milam and Bryant ask someone in the vehicle if Emmett was the right one. A "voice softer than a man's" answered "yes."

During the trial, Carolyn insisted she was not with her husband when he went to Mose's house and added how when they brought Emmett by the store for her to identify, she told her husband Emmett was not the right one. Carolyn said she saw Kimbrell standing in the store at some point but could not remember exactly when. Perhaps Kimbrell had been at the store to watch the Bryants' sleeping boys while Carolyn rode to Mose Wright's to identify Emmett?

Carolyn maintained that Roy told her the next day they had let Emmett go. The question remains, why did Roy and J.W. need to ask Carolyn to identify the boy since Emmett had already admitted to his abductors he was "the one who did the smart talk up at Money" when he was about to be taken from Mose's house.

Carolyn Bryant was never tried for kidnapping.

Scenario 4:
Sequence of Events cont…The Quonset Hut Activity

Two stops were made after Emmett's abduction from Mose Wright's house. The first stop was at Bryant's Store, discussed above. I believe the second stop was at Glendora where J.W. Milam left Hubert Clark's car and picked up his own 1955 Chevy truck which could have been parked inside the Quonset hut, especially since the truck was only three days old. Milam told Bonnie Blue they went back to Glendora and beat Emmett in a tool shed out back, something unlikely with so many people living close by, but they did go to Glendora.

Roy told in the taped conversation in 1985, they did not go to Glendora but went "through Glendora." What was the reason for going "through Glendora" since that route is out of the way if heading to Drew from Money? I believe going "through Glendora" implies stopping to make a quick trade, Hubert's car for Milam's pickup. This gives enough time for Emmett and Henry Lee Loggins to be in the Quonset hut where the voices were recorded. If the voice was Emmett, he was alive and alert, capable of begging Henry Lee

Loggins, "Help me! You're the one that brought me."

In the voice recorded in the Quonset Hut, the boy spoke with a sing-song effect, possibly an attempt to keep from stuttering. Emmett had stuttered since he had polio at six years of age. As early as the 1930's, speech therapists were aware those who stutter do not do so when singing, something Emmett would know from "doo-wopping" with his friends. Mamie, however, was convinced memorizing long passages and speeches would help Emmett with his speech problem as well as whistling when stuck on a word in order to get "unstuck."

The only person I was able to get to listen to the voice recorded in the Quonset hut who would know Emmett's voice well was Emmett's cousin Wheeler Parker. In July 2017, Reverend Parker listened to the recording while in Sumner, but Reverend Parker told me, "Honestly, Emmett stuttered so badly, I just cannot remember what his voice sounded like." I am hopeful remaining family members or friends who knew Emmett will read this book and listen to the YouTube links and be able to identify the voice recorded as "sounding like Emmett" or "not sounding like Emmett."

The story goes that after leaving Glendora, the men rode around for hours trying to find a steep bluff, the "scariest place" J.W. had ever seen, which overlooked either the Tallahatchie River or the Mississippi River. According to Milam, this would have been the perfect place where they could beat Emmett and hold him over the water to give him a good scare. When they could not find the spot and daylight began breaking, they drove to Drew to the old Shurden Plantation managed by Leslie Milam, J.W. and Roy's brother. The men needed more time to "make up their minds", as Roy told the friend in the taped interview.

Milam and Bryant probably beat Emmett intermittently during this time. Milam told Huie in the Look Magazine "confession", January 1956: "We were never able to scare him. They had just filled him so full of that poison that he was hopeless."

In the *Look* article, Milam said Emmett told them: "You bastards, I'm not afraid of you. I'm as good as you are. I've 'had' white women. My grandmother was a white woman." Milam then provided his reasoning behind the torture and murder, placing all blame on

Emmett. Willie Reed and other witnesses heard sounds of screaming and cries for help coming from the seed barn. This disproves Milam's statement in the LOOK article, "We were never able to scare him."

Scenario 5:
Surprise Witness

Between 6:00-6:30 a.m. on Sunday Morning, August 28th, eighteen-year-old Willie Reed was walking to a local store when he met a green and white Chevy pickup coming toward the Shurden Plantation. Willie noticed four white men in the cab and either two or three (his story changed) black men in the back of the truck with a boy he later identified from photographs as Emmett Till.

Willie Reed later heard screams and pleas for help coming from the barn with sounds of a terrible, torturous beating. Willie walked to Amanda Bradley's house nearby, and they listened together to the screams and sounds of human torture. According to Dr. T.R.M. Howard, civil rights activist from Mound Bayou, Willie told him he heard terrified pleas of "Mama, please save me!" and "Please, God! Don't do it again!"

Add Reed, Willie's grandfather with whom Willie lived, reported seeing J.W. Milam and Leslie Milam at the barn. J.W. Milam left the barn at one point and went to the well for a drink where Willie was getting a bucket of water. Willie noticed J.W. had a pistol on his side.

After an hour more, someone drove a tractor from the shed and J.W. Milam backed the pickup inside. A few minutes later, the pickup left with something lying in the back, covered with a tarpaulin.

Willie Reed became a surprise witness at the trial of Milam and Roy, something that scared Willie so bad, he left Mississippi right after the trial and moved north where he was hospitalized with a nervous breakdown. Willie disappeared for decades after changing his last name but resurfaced as an older adult after many of those involved had died and times were less fearful for African Americans. In 2004, Willie appeared on Keith Beauchamp's documentary *The Untold Story of Emmett Louis Till* and told what he had seen on that early morning in 1955.

Scenario 6:
White Accomplices

Although conflicting stories abound, white accomplices reported to have been with J.W. Milam and Roy Bryant when Emmett was tortured included Leslie Milam, manager on the Shurden Plantation and brother to J.W. and Roy. Years later, Leslie Milam made a deathbed confession to his pastor admitting to his part in the Till murder. Melvin Campbell, brother-in-law to J.W. Milam, was reported as being the one who shot Emmett in the head. Roy's twin brother told Carolyn "Melvin did it" and not Roy. In Roy's taped interview of 1985, he told how Hubert Clark allowed the murderers to use his car to abduct Emmett from Mose's house. Elmer Kimbrell, another friend of Milam, could have been an accomplice but there is less information about his participation. A few weeks after Milam and Bryant's trial, Kimbrell proved he was capable of murder, when he shot and killed Clinton Melton. Like his friend J.W. Milam, Kimbrell was found not guilty.

Scenario 7:
Black Accomplices

Black accomplices included Henry Lee Loggins, right hand man of J.W. Milam, who denied having been part of Emmett's kidnapping and murder. Henry's father and wife both told journalist James L. Hicks how Henry Lee Loggins was on the truck with Emmett the night he was abducted and killed. Levi "Two Tight" Collins lived with Henry Lee Loggins and his wife, and was also reported by Henry's wife and father as being on the back of Milam's truck with Emmett. Two Tight was present during the torture and was recruited later in the morning to clean the blood out of the back of J.W.'s truck and to burn Emmett's shoes. Joe Willie Hubbard and/or Oso Johnson, Jr., were both identified as being on the back of J.W.'s truck when it turned toward the barn at Drew. The two men were also seen at or near J.W.'s truck in Glendora when blood was being washed off.

Two Tight Collins and Henry Lee Loggins were wanted as witnesses in the trial of Milam and Bryant but could not be found. Many believe they were hidden in local jails, especially the jail in Charleston, but this was never proven.

Scenario 8:
After Daylight

J.W.'s green and white pickup was back at home in Glendora by late morning August 28th, with blood dripping off the back and thick, jelly like clots pooled under the truck. When asked by a local black man about the blood, J.W. Milam answered he had killed a deer even though it was not deer season. Another possible addition to this story was the uncovering of the corpse under the tarpaulin when J.W. showed a questioning black man what happens when "niggers" get too smart for their own good.

Two Tight Collins and Oso Johnson were both seen around Milam's bloody truck on Sunday morning, and Two Tight took hours burning something in a barrel behind Milam's house. Emmett's crepe soled shoes had been mistakenly left in Leslie Milam's car and not buried with the bloody clothes. Crepe soles do not burn and this caused a problem for Two Tight. At one point, Two Tight was reported as telling a passerby the shoe lying on the ground belonged to Emmett Till.

Scenario 9:
The Cotton Gin Fan

The seventy-pound gin fan used to weigh Emmett's body down was taken from the Glendora Cotton Gin, formally titled Mississippi Cottonseed Products Company and deeded to M.E. Lowe, December 30, 1950. The gin and all property associated with the gin were transferred to Martha B. Lowe July 19, 1956. This information is based on a warranty deed signed July 16, 1956, and recorded in Sumner Courthouse. The Glendora Gin with the Quonset hut were located beside J.W. Milam's house. The old gin now houses the Emmett Till Historical and Intrepid Center and is symbolic of the life giving force Emmett's death contributed to the Civil Rights Movement. Henry Lee Loggins' son Mayor Johnny B. Thomas serves as the Executive Director of the center. Mayor Thomas plans to write a book about his father's involvement in the Till murder.

Elmer Kimbrell worked at the Glendora Gin and is probably the one who secured the gin fan to tie around Emmett's neck.

Scenario 10:
Henry Lee Loggins' Part in Emmett's Murder

Although Henry Lee Loggins spent the rest of his life denying any part in Emmett's lynching, he is said to have confessed to his part right before his death. The deep male voice recorded in the Quonset hut is thought to be Henry Lee Loggins explaining to Emmett why he took part in the kidnapping and why he cannot help the boy, something Loggins showed remorse for in the voice recording. This belief is based on a comparison of the voice recorded in the Quonset hut and Loggins' voice in the documentary *The Untold Story of Emmett Louis Till,* as well as in "Emmett Till Case at '60 Minutes", CBS 2005 broadcast.

In May, 2017, Mayor Thomas listened to the voice recorded on February 26, 2017, but said he could not hear it well enough to identify it as his father. This took place inside one of the unfinished rooms inside the Quonset hut after it was enclosed. The Quonset hut serves other purposes now as part of the Emmett Till Historical and Intrepid Center.

Henry Lee Loggins died in Dayton, Ohio in 2009.

Scenario 11:
Dumping Emmett's Body

Conflicting reports suggest two different sites where Emmett's body was dumped after his murder, according to the Emmett Till Memory Project. In the *Look* article in January 1956, Milam claimed Emmett's body was thrown directly into the Tallahatchie River, about

3.5 miles south of Sharkey Road on River Road out from Glendora. In this case, the body would have traveled eight miles to be picked up in the Tallahatchie River where stated in the trial.

The second theory is Emmett's body was thrown into Black Bayou from the bridge on the edge of Glendora, a theory supported by Mayor Johnny B. Thomas whose father was Henry Lee Loggins. For the body to be discovered where it was reported at the trial, Emmett's body would have had to travel ten miles from the bridge, something extremely difficult considering the heavy gin fan attached to Emmett's body. However, if the body was recovered where the bayou meets the Tallahatchie River, the site marked earlier by an Emmett Till Memorial Commission, the body only had to float 1.8 miles, much more believable considering the amount of mud picked up making the gin fan even heavier.

In *The Untold Story of Emmett Louis Till*, Henry Lee Loggins, while vehemently denying taking part in Emmett's torture and murder, made a slip of the tongue when telling what a "woman named Mary" told him. "I know nothing about it, no more than what was told me," Loggins insisted, emphasizing the word "told." "She said J.W. and them went over to Money and killed a boy and put him in the river *(stutters)*... Well, it wasn't a river . . . it was Black Bayou."

The official site where Emmett's body was thrown into water will never be known for sure. If paranormal evidence is taken into consideration, Black Bayou Bridge is the logical choice. Two white feathers were left here during two separate visits, two months apart. The first white feather, a large one from an egret or crane, floated under the bridge where six of us stood watching it follow the same path Emmett's body took floating downstream, and the second feather was found on the bridge itself. Add to this the chuckle heard at four different locations including the bridge when white feather three was found, and it appears the bridge was being identified (by someone) as significant. Also, the bridge was close to J.W. Milam's house and the gin where the fan was obtained. With the arrival of daylight came the urgency to get rid of the body as quickly as possible.

*UPDATE FROM DR. SUE: On September 7, 2017, my friend Hilda and I went back to Black Bayou Bridge, a haunting spot that draws both of us to it. As we walked up on the bridge, I explained to Hilda how no one is sure Black Bayou Bridge is where Milam and Bryant dumped Emmett's body. I then told her how I know it is because of Emmett's two feathers and because of his chuckle. While on the bridge, I spoke aloud telling Emmett I had finished his book, and I asked him if he wanted me to add anything to it. Two more chuckles were recorded, one heard right beside the video camera with no amplification needed to hear it. The chuckles did not come from Hilda or me, and we were the only ones on the bridge. For me, this validates Black Bayou Bridge as being the location where J.W. Milam and Roy Bryant dumped Emmett's body. Watch YouTube link: https://youtu.be/ns5NRDdAlDY and hear the last two chuckles from Emmett before I sent the final copy of the book to my publisher.

Scenario 12:
Emmett's Injuries

In 2005, after the FBI reopened the Till case, Emmett's body was exhumed and an autopsy was performed. Through dental records and DNA evidence, the body was identified as that of Emmett Till. Sheriff Clarence Strider had used the failure to identify the body as Till to sway the jury in favor of acquittal of Roy Bryant and J.W. Milam.

The autopsy determined cause of death to be a gunshot wound to the head, by a .45 Colt pistol, the gun J.W. Milam carried. Other findings recorded in the FBI autopsy report included: "extensive and dramatic fractures of the skull with areas of bone missing; metallic fragments in the cranium; vertical symphyseal *(symphysis)* fracture of thyroid cartilage; distal left femur fracture; fractures in both wrist bones; one tooth knocked out; lead fragments found identified as from a .45 caliber pistol." The death of Emmett Till was ruled a homicide—no surprise.

Other facts known concerning the physical torture of Emmett

included: his left eye had been gouged out and was hanging on his cheek; his skull was split and part of his brain fell into the boat when his body was lifted from the water; part of one ear lobe was missing as if the ear had been clipped.

"No evidence of wounds made by a drill were found on Till's body; no 'scraping wounds' or 'awl' wounds were found on the body at the time of the autopsy." No signs of castration or attempted castration were noted.

In Bonnie Blue's book based on Milam's phone interviews with her, J.W. Milam told her he had used a rusted drill bit and bore into Emmett's head while he was still alive; castration was also mentioned, something not approved by the other men in the barn at Drew. Two Tight Collins had told people the hole in Emmett's head was made by a drill bit but this was not proven by the autopsy. The FBI autopsy maintained the hole through Emmett's head was made by a .45 Colt automatic pistol shot directly through the skull above the left ear.

Scenario 13:
Possible KKK Involvement

Susan Orr-Klopfer gives an account of a seventeen-year-old girl who said Milam and Bryant came to her parents' house the night of the murder, something which conflicts with the reported time of the abduction and torture according to witness testimonies. One other comment by the girl does ring of possible truth: "After the trial, the only support for Milam and Bryant came from the Klan because they were members."

The FBI never proved any connection of Milam and Bryant with the Klan, but the psychic Livie did see a possible connection. Livie's disclosure of secret meetings held at Bryant's Store, "men meetings", certainly sounds like Klan activity.

Scenario 14:
Last Breath Taken

Where did Emmett Till take his last breath? Most researchers believe Emmett died in the seed barn at Drew. He certainly sustained injuries severe enough to cause death at the barn, but due to the paranormal occurrences captured and recorded in the Quonset hut at Glendora on February 26, 2017, I believe Emmett, though unconscious, was still alive when his body was placed in the back of J.W. Milam's pickup and covered with a tarpaulin. The thought of Emmett dying in the Quonset hut never entered my mind until I spoke aloud to Frank, "This is where he died, Frank; this is where he died." The loud bang recorded on my video camera could have been when Milam, or whoever, shot a bullet through Emmett's head. (Compare the shot in the video with the YouTube listed in the Appendix giving the sound of the same type pistol being fired).

After a loud bang, a voice that sounded like Emmett but gravelly said, "This is it." This was in answer to my, "This is where he died, Frank." This would have been residual activity, a playback of what happened in 1955, but it seemed to be answering my conversation with Frank which would make it an intelligent interaction.

Perhaps Sheriff Strider was right after all in insisting Emmett was murdered in Tallahatchie County but this, along with everything else, is still open to conjecture.

Conclusion

The year was 1955. The era was Jim Crow at its worst! Today, many who still hold animosity and prejudice in their hearts for black people chide me with: "Why are you dredging up the past? All it does is make people angry!"

This book is about Emmett Till, a fourteen-year-old child who was lynched for whistling at a white woman. Lynching happened then, and lynching and hate crimes still happen today. No one should be guilty of thinking like murderer Roy Bryant, who in a radio interview in 1992 stated: "Emmett Till is dead! Why can't you just let him stay dead!"

Emmett Till will never die! In 2008, the Emmett Till Unsolved Civil Rights Crimes Act was passed and the "Till Bill" became law. Many old Civil Rights cases were reopened and murderers were brought to justice. In 2016, the act was reauthorized and strengthened adding additional years to the timeline for solving civil rights cold cases. Collaboration between the FBI, the Department of Justice, and state and local law enforcement was also strengthened with reauthorization.

Emmett's mother Mamie Till-Mobley was right. God had so much planned for Emmett Till, even in death, his life goes on!

Doves, white feathers, chuckles, knock-knocks, voices—what does it all mean? And what am I—a seventy-two-year-old grandmother, retired educator, and author supposed to do with it all? Now that I have finished writing this very difficult book, will I finally be able to relax, sleep—move on? How will I know if the book was what I was meant to do, the reason for the white feathers gifted me by Emmett? I wish I had the answers to these questions still haunting my every waking moment and believe me—there are far too many waking moments in my life!

In Keith's documentary *The Untold Story of Emmett Louis Till*, I was in awe of Mamie Till-Mobley (Mother Mobley). Her bravery in the face of the death of her son could only be the result of tremendous faith in God. Mamie proved this in her statement at the end of the documentary where she tells of receiving a vision from God:

> Without the shedding of blood, there is no redemption, and I do know that the Lord appeared to me in a vision and He told me Emmett was not mine; that he belonged to Him; and that God had chosen him for this particular mission.

Many people who read of my experiences with Emmett Till will immediately discredit me and criticize my methods and this is okay. Some will try to explain away each piece of video evidence and each voice recorded in an attempt to convert the illogical into logical. Others will take the easy way out and say, "I really could not hear anything."

Did I go seeking paranormal verification of what happened in the early morning hours of August 28, 1955? Not likely, since I had so little information about Emmett Till in February 2017 when this all began. But something happened in that Quonset hut, something life changing, something I can never forget. Will I ever be able to put Emmett completely behind me? Probably not. Nothing making this big of an impression could ever be pushed to the back shelf of my mind.

What I do know is I will return to the sites of Emmett's abduction, torture, and murder, maybe not as often, but I will return and maybe even volunteer at the Emmett Till Interpretive Center if director Patrick Weems ever needs or wants me. But from now on, before I leave the sites in the Delta, especially the bridge at Black Bayou and the shed at Drew, my last words will always be for Emmett:

"I'm here—giving love."

Dr. Sue

In Retrospect…

Home of Mose and Elizabeth Wright's Neighbors in 1955

The door above remained closed to Elizabeth Wright when she fled across the dark fields to her nearest (white) neighbor's house in the early morning hours of August 28, 1955, seeking help after her nephew Emmett Till was abducted. The closed door could have become the symbol, the rallying cry, against Mississippi's *Closed Society*, the title of the controversial book written by University of Mississippi history professor James W. Silver in 1963. Emmett's murder caused many Mississippians to question the old ways, bringing about a new awareness of the wrongdoing against African Americans. However, the voices of conscience remained silent for a few more decades, drowned out by fear of retaliation from the Klan or White Citizens Council, or from fear of social ostracism by neighbors.

If only people could have been like long time Sumner resident Betty Pearson, mistress of her husband's Delta Rainbow Plantation. Betty was not a white woman ahead of her time as many thought, but she was a woman in tune with her own sense of morality and fairness, an activist for equal rights for black Americans. This philosophy went against the beliefs of almost everyone in her state including her beloved father. Betty, incensed with the violence against blacks, culminating in the murder of Emmett Till, secured journalist passes for herself and her friend Florence Mars, and the two women were present every day of Milam and Bryant's trial.

Rainbow Plantation became a refuge and a safe place for journalists and civil rights activists in the last half of the 20th century. While active in the Human Relations Council which sought to open communications between blacks and whites, Betty also became a "card-carrying member" of the NAACP.

In the midst of helping her husband Bill in running Rainbow, Betty often took part in civil rights demonstrations such as the march commemorating the death of Dr. Martin Luther King, Jr., in Memphis. Betty took the responsibility for helping black residents in her community in registering to vote or in humanitarian efforts.

In 1959, Betty joined the Mississippi Advisory Committee to the United States Civil Rights Commission, and in 2006, she became a member of the Emmett Till Commission. Betty was trusted by both blacks and whites in Sumner and in Tallahatchie County in general.

Through all of her crusades, Betty Pearson never forgot those who suffered the most in the fight for equal rights. She stated in *Delta Rainbow*, "I do not compare my experience with that of the true heroines of the civil rights movement, those brave black women who were arrested and beaten time after time, only to come back and try once more to register to vote."

Betty and Bill Pearson are now in their nineties and live in California near their daughter.

Former home of Betty and Bill Pearson in Sumner, MS

Finding My WAY—with the Help of Friends and a Son!

Dr. Sue on Black Bayou Bridge

Hilda—thinking and feeling on Black Bayou Bridge

Belinda and Frank drove all the way from Georgia to the Mississippi Delta! Belinda found the first white feather and was with Dr. Sue when three of the four white feathers were found.

Kelly Paris Photography—Kelly sees each shot within the context of the story!

Help in writing the murder scene comes from the North, in Connecticut where Dr. Sue's writer son Jeff Gentry pounds out the gruesome details of Emmett's murder. Jeff's description is based on credible research by noted historians, on the FBI Autopsy Report from 2005, on interviews with Milam and Bryant before their deaths, and on paranormal evidence recorded at five major Emmett Till sites in the Delta.

New Friends

(Top) Keith Beauchamp with Dr. Sue and Keith's parents Edgar and Ceola Beauchamp who were Keith's executive producers on his documentary *The Untold Story of Emmett Louis Till; (Bottom)* Keith pictured at the panel discussion at Sumner Courthouse, summer 2017.

(Top) Wheeler Parker, Emmett's cute cousin Johnna, Dr. Sue and Keith; *(Bottom)* Ceola with Emmett's cousin Priscilla (mom to Johnna) at Sumner Courthouse, July 2017

(Top) Dr. Sue with Reverend Wheeler Parker who was with Emmett during the wolf whistle incident and when Emmett was kidnapped; *(Bottom)* Panel discussion at Sumner Courthouse, June 2017; (Carolyn Webb, pictured on panel with Wheeler and Keith, was on the first Emmett Till Commission in Tallahatchie County, and Carolyn was a long time friend of Betty Pearson).

Dr. Sue presents Keith Beauchamp with an award winning photo, taken by photographer Milly Moorhead West in 1983. Milly photographed the old FBI poster behind the counter in a drug store owned by Aaron Henry in Clarksdale. Aaron Henry was a former NAACP Director for Mississippi. The poster had been circulated during Freedom Summer, 1964, when civil rights workers Michael Schwerner, James Chaney, and Andrew Goodman were reported missing in Neshoba County. The bodies of the three young men were discovered a few weeks later in an earthen dam.

Since Keith Beauchamp is a crusader in solving civil rights cold cases, Dr. Sue felt it was fitting for Keith to have the print she bought from her photographer friend Milly in 1983. Keith's many attributes, to name just a few, include: filmmaker for *The Untold Story of Emmett Louis Till, 2005*; host of the "Injustice Files" on

Investigation Discovery; "Murder in Black and White" documentary for TV One, 2008; and filmmaker and Executive Producer for new movie *Till* with Director Whoopi Goldberg and an all star production team.

Milly's photograph "Schwerner, Chaney, and Goodman, 1983" is part of the permanent collections "Icons of Freedom" exhibit in Mississippi's Museum of Art and in Ogden Museum of Southern Art in New Orleans, Louisiana. The photograph was also on exhibit in the Cocoran Museum of Art in Washington, D.C.

Through the Camera Lens of Kelly Paris Photography

Seed Barn at Drew (from another angle)

Glendora, Mississippi

Main Street
Just passin' time!

Frank

Frank, also known as Pooky, describes growing up in Glendora and working on a white plantation: "You got out there in that field and you do what he *(boss)* tell you to do and you got no problems...but you get to talkin' back...yeah, you gon' have problems...he probably gon' put you off the place! Where you gon' go? Where you gon' go? You ain't got no place to go!"

Oldest house in Glendora…Frank's house

The Wisdom of Frank from Glendora as told to Dr. Sue

Frank on R.E.S.P.E.C.T: "You learn your manners from home. Don't matter what color, what race…you learn your respect from your mama and 'em. And if you ain't got no respect for yourself, how someone else gon' respect you?"

Frank on the Importance of Talking to Each Other: "I appreciate the conversation we are having 'cause it's positive. Ain't talking about that negative stuff. Everything we talk about is positive…it might be in the past…might be in the future, but we enjoyin' the conversation."

Little John, another face defined by time passed in Glendora, MS
The pleasant little man's face tells many stories.

Glendora, MS, major site in murder of Emmett Till and once home to murderer J.W. Milam, still looks much as it did in 1955. Dr. Sue was principal of Black Bayou Elementary School here in the mid 1990's. The school is now a Head Start Center.

Grayson M.B. Church
Glendora, MS

Across the Tracks in Glendora

Old River Site sign, full of bullet holes, was removed when the new sign was installed and was stored in the Emmett Till Interpretative Center in Sumner. The new sign is now riddled with bullet holes just like the old one.

East Money Church of God in Christ

Dr. Sue hopes to catch voices on her video camera, but all is silent at East Money Church of God in Christ, home church of Mose and Elizabeth Wright. Mose Wright often preached here, and Mose prepared to conduct Emmett's funeral service here a few hours after his body was found in the Tallahatchie River. Tallahatchie Sheriff H.C. Strider ordered Emmett to be buried quickly—reason unclear, but the burial was halted by Emmett's grieving mother's orders to send her son's body home to Chicago. The church needs to be saved as an important Emmett Till site.

Cemetery at East Money Church of God in Christ is where Emmett's body was brought for burial. The grave was dug, but the burial was halted by Leflore County Sheriff George Smith after Emmett's mother Mamie ordered her son's body to be shipped to Chicago for burial.

Drew, Mississippi: "The mural says it all!"

Sumner, Mississippi

About the Front Cover Art

White Feathers from Emmett

Choosing the picture for the front cover proved to be an overwhelming task since my photographer Kelly gave me so many wonderful choices. Should it be the bridge with its historic Pony Truss construction, its rusted iron rails standing as testament to where Emmett's body was dumped in the summer of 1955? No, the bridge serves as the back cover.

Perhaps, it should be the shed at Drew where Emmett called for his mother and for God, pleading with them to make the torture stop. Now spirit children play and sing in opposite ends of the old barn—the boy (Emmett?) chuckles, and the little girl sings, "The rain can't go…I can go!"

Or should I choose the stately old courthouse in Sumner where justice was not served—where the Mississippi State flag flapped in the wind as if applauding the decision made by the jurors in 1955. As the defendants stood listening to the jury foreman announce "not guilty", the murderers' boot treads still held traces of the blood of Emmett Till.

But when Kelly sent me the photograph of the ruins of Bryant Store at Money, my senses told me this was the photograph symbolizing it all. Very little remains of the old store. The brick walls crumble into obscurity, reminding onlookers of the life of Roy Bryant after 1955. The old store is dead! The murderers and their accomplices are dead!

Yet beside the nearly razed building, a magnolia tree stands tall and lovely to behold like the Hedy Lamarr lookalike who worked in her husband Roy's store in the summer of 1955. Each May, the branches hold exquisite, sweet-smelling blossoms symbolic of a youthful Carolyn who won many beauty contests—before Roy Bryant. I am still angry with Carolyn even though I know the young wife suffered from mental and physical abuse at the hands of her high-tempered, heavy drinking husband Roy. In Devery S. Anderson's book, he gives the complaints listed in the divorce papers filed by Carolyn as "Habitual cruel and inhuman treatment" of Carolyn, along with Roy's "habitual drunkenness." Roy Bryant did not dispute the complaints and the divorce was granted.

Carolyn feared her husband and followed his orders just as

Henry Loggins and Two Tight Collins feared "the boss" J.W. Milam and obeyed him without question. So many wrongs! So many opportunities missed to help a fourteen-year-old boy escape!

But the crumbling walls and stately magnolia tree are not what caught my eye. Rusted barbed wire, three strands wide, warn trespassers of an ominous past.

The store is where the tale of horror began. The barbed wire is how it ended.

Dr. Sue

Magnolia blossoms beside the vine covered remains of Bryant Store speak of sweeter days—now distant memories.

This store served its community well—until a murderer bought it! Now the walls crumble like the lives destroyed in a nightmare tale beginning with an impulsive young boy's wolf whistle.

About the Back Cover Art

The back cover pictures the haunting Black Bayou Bridge. Emmett left two white feathers here, including the final feather. From the bridge, I watched a magnificent white egret standing in the water's edge until it took flight, following the route Emmett's body traveled that August. The egret's flight path curved with the bayou and disappeared when it reached the Tallahatchie River. But soon the egret returned, but this time the bird flapped much smaller wings in rapid movement as it climbed toward heaven. The egret, transformed into a small white dove, disappeared in the billowy clouds above us. This was a final message for me: "Emmett is at peace. Your quest is over. Time to write."

Dr. Sue

YouTube Links in Book

Many of the voices are faint and hard for untrained ears to decipher. For best results, use external speakers and listen several times in order to hear each voice. The YouTube links for *White Feathers from Emmett* are listed in the order presented in the narrative. (All videos are unlisted in YouTube)

1) https://youtu.be/f7g7mYhbUzc

2) https://youtu.be/RyJO4iTCFn4

3) https://youtu.be/1oc4M7YLhc4

4) https://youtu.be/27F3mZ2XldY

5) https://youtu.be/3tOLBpUc2HI

6) https://youtu.be/2GfwIHj8J54

7) https://youtu.be/xmMqh-gKRFg

8) https://youtu.be/ns5NRDdAlDY

REWARD OFFERED!

Emmett Till's silver signet ring originally belonged to his father Louis Till. After his death in 1945, the ring was sent to Mamie who saved it for her son. Emmett wore it for the first time on his trip to Mississippi in August 1955. Emmett's uncle Mose Wright identified the body found in the Tallahatchie River on August 31, 1955, as Emmett Till because of the silver ring still on his finger. The ring was admitted as evidence in the trial of J.W. Milam and Roy Bryant and was identified by Emmett's mother Mamie Till-Mobley. The ring disappeared during or after the trial of J.W. Milam and Roy Bryant.

The silver ring has great meaning for the Civil Rights Movement and for history in general as well as being important to Emmett's family. Simeon Wright, Emmett's cousin who was in bed with Emmett when he was abducted, was promised this ring by Emmett, but this never came to fruition. On September 4, 2017, Simeon passed away. I was so in hopes the ring would be turned in for the reward offered before he passed.

If anyone has information about the ring's whereabouts, or information that can lead to its recovery, please contact me by email at drsueclifton@gmail.com. Monetary reward is available but only if information results in the ring's return. If and when the ring is found and returned, it will be returned to Emmett's family in honor of Simeon Wright. The family will make the decision of what to do with the ring.

No legal consequences are foreseen and no questions will be asked since the ring disappeared so long ago and was likely taken by a person now deceased.

                                      Dr. Sue

Appendix

Works Consulted

American Experience. *The Murder of Emmett Till. PBS Special* ... https://youtu.be/Uh3NgRmvlZY. Accessed 14 August 2017.

Anderson, Devery S. *Emmett Till: The Murder that Shocked the World and Propelled the Civil Rights Movement.* Jackson: University Press of Mississippi, 2015.

Beauchamp, Keith. Executive Producer and Director. *Murder in Black and White: Lamar Smith.* TV One, LLC, 2008.

Beauchamp, Keith. Filmmaker. *The Untold Story of Emmett Louis Till.* ThinkFilm, 2005.

Beauchamp, Keith. Personal Interview. Telephone. 15 Apr. 2017.

Blue, Bonnie. *Emmett Till's Secret Witness: FBI Confidential Source Speaks.* Park Forrest, IL: BL Richey, 2013.

"Colt 45 Pistol Sound Effects One Shot! Pistol Sound Effects Free Download." https://youtu.be/w2FDpiG09mE. Accessed 6 Sept. 2017.

Curry, Constance and Marian Wright Edelman. *Silver Rights: The story of the Carter family's brave decision to send their children to an all-white school and claim their civil rights.* Algonquin Books, 1996.

"Emmett Till Case, Part II." *60 Minutes* CBS 2005. *YouTube,* YouTube, 13 Sept. 2012, www.youtube.com/watch?v=WQC5WJMYaug. Accessed 14 Aug. 2017.

"Emmett Till Memory Project." *Emmett Till Memory Project,* tillmemoryproject.com. Accessed 14 Aug. 2017, 6 Sept. 2017.

FBI Report and *Emmett Till Murder and Trial Transcript for Roy Bryant and J.W. Milam Murder Trial,* Sumner, MS, 1955. 475 pages total, 2006.

Garth Brooks Shares Updated Poignant 'We Shall Be Free' Video.

Vimeo, Accessed 5 Sept. 2017.

Lamar Smith – Notice to Close File. Dept. of Justice, Civil Rights Division, 2010, updated 2016.

Huie, William B. "The Shocking Story of Approved Killing in Mississippi," *Look*. 24 Jan. 1956.

Jackson, Ruth. *Whore's Lake*. Xlibris, 2010.

Jones, Maya A. "Congress passes Emmett Till Unsolved Civil Rights Crimes Reauthorization Act." *The Undefeated*, Dec. 14, 2016.

King James Study Bible. Thomas Nelson, Inc., 1985.

Orr-Klopfer, Susan. *The Emmett Till Book*. Lulu, 2005.

Orr-Klopfer, Susan. Emmett Till Blog: Murder in Mississippi Delta; Civil Rights Cold Cases; Parallels Trayvon Martin. http://emmett-till.blogspot.com/. *Accessed 18 Aug. 2017.*

Parker, Wheeler. "Panel Discussion on Emmett Till." National Endowment for the Arts in conjunction with Delta State School of Education. 22 June 2017 and July 2017, Sumner, MS, Sumner Courthouse.

Reynolds, Gretchen. "The Stuttering Doctor's Monster Study." *New York Times Magazine*, March 16, 2003.

Silver, James W. *Mississippi: The Closed Society*. New York: Harcourt, Brace, & World, Inc., 1963-1966.

Thomas, Johnny B. "My Father Helped Kill Emmett Till: Healing from the Sins of Thy Father, Part 1 of 2." *YouTube*, YouTube, 31 Dec. 2012, www.youtube.com/watch?v=XkthhlDJP5Y. Accessed 14 Aug. 2017.

Thomason, Sally Palmer and Jean Carter Fisher. *Delta Rainbow: The Irrepressible Betty Bobo Pearson*. Jackson: University Press, 2016.

Till-Mobley, Mamie, and Chris Benson. *Death of Innocence: The Story of the Hate Crime that Changed America*. New York: Ballantine Books, 2005.

Tyson, Timothy B. *The Blood of Emmett Till*. New York: Simon & Schuster, 2017.

Warranty Deed granting ownership of Glendora Cotton Gin (Mississippi Cottonseed Products Company) to M.E. Lowe. Book 100, pp. 125-6 of Deed and Trust Records, Second

Judicial District, Tallahatchie County, Mississippi. December 30, 1950.

Warranty Deed granting ownership of Glendora Cotton Gin to Martha B. Lowe. Book 118, p. 165 of Deed and Trust Records, Second Judicial District, Tallahatchie County. July 19, 1956.

Wright, Simeon, and Herb Boyd. *Simeon's Story: An Eyewitness Account of the Kidnapping of Emmett Till.* Chicago: Lawrence Hill Books, 2010.

Longer Quotations with Sources

NOTE: Unless otherwise acknowledged within the text of *White Feathers from Emmett*, references for direct quotations and page numbers are noted in parentheses after each resource below.

1) Chapter 1 in *White Feathers for Emmett Till*, Quote by Simeon Wright: "I enjoyed the sound of his voice; when Bobo talked, he stuttered, and more so when he got excited, but he used that to capture your attention." (From *Simeon's Story*, p. 43)

2) Chapters 1 & 11 in *White Feathers...*: Quotes by Mamie Till-Mobley from *Death of Innocence*, page numbers given at end of each quote:

   a) "I heard more chickens crossing more roads, and knock-knock this and knock-knock that." (p. 40)

   b) "For Emmett, life was laughter and laughter was life-giving. There was so much joy in his carefree world that he just wanted to share with everyone around him. He did it the only way a young boy knows how to do it. He made people laugh." (pp. 40-41)

   c) "There came a point in the middle of everything, as I was listening to the speakers, when I had a sensation. It was something I could just barely make out. Something fluttering somewhere. It seemed like it was in the corner of my eye, at the edge of my awareness. As my eye darted to get a better look and as my head turned to follow, the image seemed to move, just ahead of my gaze, always just a flutter ahead like that, always on the borderline

between conscious and subconscious. It would happen like that over and over again. And it looked to me like a dove. I wanted to see it fully, but never could. It would always move away just when I'd turn my full attention to it. I came to realize that it was a sign. The dove. A sign of peace. A sign from God." (p. 144)
   d) "You say you could beat their what?" (p. 82)
   e) "How do you give a crash course in hatred to a boy who has only known love?" (p. 102)
3) In Conclusion from *White Feathers...*, Quote by Mamie Till-Mobley: Without the shedding of blood, there is no redemption, and I do know that the Lord appeared to me in a vision and He told me Emmett was not mine; that he belonged to Him; and that God had chosen him for this particular mission. (Quote from end of *The Untold Story of Emmett Louis Till*)
4) Chapter 2 in *White Feathers...* "Nothing that boy did could ever justify what happened to him." (Quote by Carolyn Bryant Donham, *The Blood of Emmett Till*, p. 7)
5) Chapter 5 in *White Feathers...*: "Emmett Till ruined my life." (Quote attributed to Roy Bryant, Emmett Till Memory Project, Roy Bryant Gravesite description)
6) In Retrospect in White Feathers...: Quote by Betty Pearson: "I do not compare my experience with that of the true heroines of the civil rights movement, those brave black women who were arrested and beaten time after time, only to come back and try once more to register to vote." (*Delta Rainbow*, p. 109)
7) Chapter 6 in *White Feathers...*: "Well, what else could we do? He was hopeless. I'm no bully; I never hurt a nigger in my life. I like niggers -- in their place -- I know how to work 'em. But I just decided it was time a few people got put on notice. As long as I live and can do anything about it, niggers are gonna stay in their place..." (J.W. Milam's statement to Huie, *Look Magazine*, January 1956).
8) Chapter 12 in *White Feathers...* "After the trial, the only support for Milam and Bryant came from the Klan because

they were member." (Klopfer, *The Emmett Till Book*, p. 8)
9) Front Cover Art explanation in *White Feathers*…Contents of divorce papers filed by Carolyn Bryant: "habitual cruelty and inhuman treatment" and "habitual drunkenness", (Devery Anderson, p. 277)

Emmett Till Memory Project

Emmett Till Memory Project (ETMP) was created by a collaborative team: Davis Houck and Pablo Correa of Florida State University, Chris Spielvogel of Penn State's Center for Democratic Deliberation, and Patrick Weems of the Emmett Till Interpretive Center. The interactive application takes full advantage of the latest technology in providing map and GPS locations for 51 sites important to the Emmett Till murder. Not only does it locate the sites for teachers, students, tourists, historians, writers, and anyone interested in following the path of the Emmett Till lynching, but the project includes a description of what happened at each site and updates information on topics such as vandalism and any new developments.

The Emmett Till Memory Project is readily available and easily accessed either by use of a smart phone app through Google Field Trips or by using the website. For more information, visit www.tillmemoryproject.com.

About the Author

Dr. Sue Clifton is a retired principal and teacher, a fly fisher, a paranormal investigator, and a published author. Dr. Sue cannot remember a time when she did not write beginning with two plays published at age sixteen. Her writing career was placed on hold while she traveled the world with her husband Woody in his career as well as with her own career as a teacher and principal in Mississippi, Alberta (Canada), Alaska, New Zealand, and on the Northern Cheyenne Reservation in Montana. The places Dr. Sue has lived provide rich background and settings for the novels she creates.

Dr. Sue now divides her time among Mississippi, Montana, and Arkansas and enjoys traveling with Woody and the grandchildren as well as with her national 9000-member women's fly fishing group, Sisters On the Fly.

Dr. Sue is the author of nine published books including two paranormal mysteries and two nonfiction books with Double Dragon Publishing and five works of fiction in her "Daughters of Parrish Oaks" series with The Wild Rose Press. In addition to writing, Dr. Sue presents to many groups including schools. To schedule a presentation by Dr. Sue, contact her by email at: drsueclifton@gmail.com.

Visit Dr. Sue at: http://www.drsueclifton.com

Or at Novels by Dr. Sue Clifton on Facebook

About the Co-Author.

Jeff Gentry's field of work is in safety management in large commercial and industrial construction projects. Jeff graduated from Columbia Southern University with a Bachelor's Degree in Occupational Safety. When not performing responsibilities as Safety Manager, Jeff enjoys spending time with his wife Lee and their three daughters. Jeff is an avid fly fisher and enjoys the great trout streams of the West as well as the White River in Arkansas.

Although Jeff is not new to writing, *White Feathers from Emmett* is his first time to be published as a co-author. His specialty is writing about wars and the horrible effects of wars on refugees, especially children. He is presently working on a book of short stories but plans to continue writing with his mother Dr. Sue on other projects.

About the Photographer.

Kelly Paris is a wife, mother of one son and three daughters, and grandmother to four. Kelly graduated from Northwest Community College with an Associate's Degree. While at college, she met and married Ping Pong Paris.

Kelly's interest in photography began over thirty years ago and has grown into a passion and a profession. Her growing up in Tallahatchie County where the Emmett Till murder took place made her the perfect choice for photographing the Emmett Till sites for this book. Kelly's love of photography is evident in the unique way she sets up each shot, placing the subject in proper perspective to enhance the story.

For more information about Kelly, or to book a photo shoot, message her on her Facebook page: Kelly D Paris Photography.

Other Books by Dr. Sue Clifton with Double Dragon Publishing

Through the Eyes of Angel Leigh

J.K. Puck, the School That Doesn't Suck

Freeze Tag!

"Where the WAY leads, I will follow!"
Dr. Sue

www.ingramcontent.com/pod-product-compliance
Lightning Source LLC
Chambersburg PA
CBHW070702100426
42735CB00039B/2430